P9-CFM-745

INVOLVEMENT BY INVITATION

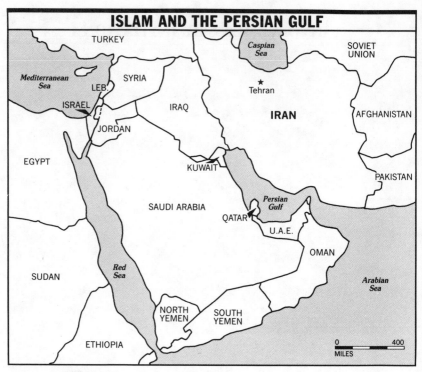

ISLAM AND THE PERSIAN GULF

Courtesy of the *Washington Post.*

INVOLVEMENT BY INVITATION

American Strategies of Containment in Iran

Kuross A. Samii

THE PENNSYLVANIA STATE UNIVERSITY PRESS
University Park and London

Dedicated to the memory of

Robert E. Osgood

Library of Congress Cataloging-in-Publication Data

Samii, Kuross A.
Involvement by invitation.

Bibliography: p.
Includes index.
1. United States—Foreign relations—Iran.
2. Iran—Foreign relations—United States.
3. United States—Foreign relations—Soviet Union.
4. Soviet Union—Foreign relations—United States
I. Title. II. Title: Containment in Iran.
E183.8.I7S24   1987   327.73055   86-43035
ISBN 0-271-00490-8

When men cannot observe, they don't have ideas; they have obsessions. When people live instinctive lives, something like a collective amnesia steadily blurs the past.

V. S. Naipaul
India: A Wounded Civilization
1977

Contents

Preface

The most expressive face in the assembled gathering at the inauguration of Ronald Reagan on January 20, 1981, belonged to Jimmy Carter. After several sleepless nights waiting for the release of American hostages from Iran, an exhausted Jimmy Carter had to struggle to keep his eyes open and maintain his composure. There were no traces of the smile that had helped send him to the White House four years earlier. There were only the remains of a man consumed by a crisis he never fully understood—by foreign enemies who depicted him as the unholy symbol of American imperialism, and by domestic opponents who described him as the purveyor of defeatism, decline, and despair.

For sheer drama, the maddening frustration that sealed the fate of Jimmy Carter had no parallel in American history, and no playwright would have dared to produce a plot so debilitating, so absurd, and yet so final in affirming the power of propaganda and the human proclivity toward bigotry. On one side of the angry divide, there stood a clergyman, an interpreter of God's will, preaching hatred and delivering the malediction that the American government was responsible for all the confusion and the anguish of the Islamic world. On the other side, there was the President of the United States, visibly at a loss as to how he had acquired such a vindictive enemy, but allowing the State Department to portray the takeover of the American Embassy in Tehran, not as a symbolic act of terrorism by the Iranian revolutionaries, but as a direct manifestation of Persian and Islamic character.

Such a display of mutual ignorance would not have been possible without blurring the past and developing a collective amnesia toward history. The self-blinding process that made the Iranian militants try to justify their criminal acts with the pretext of the Shah's admission to the United States had already compelled them to forget the positive aspects of American involvement in their country, which, since 1942, had included a continuous stream of financial, military, educational, and technical assistance. Also forgotten was the role of the United States in saving Iran from Soviet aggression in 1946 as well as the subsequent security arrangements, which, in later years, prevented a Soviet domination of Iran and preserved the Islamic shrines from whence the Muslim militants were to initiate their revolution. Unencumbered by facts and unfettered by history, the Iranian militants chose to dwell on the negatives to fortify their own paranoia, and to imbue the people of Iran with their own anxious understanding that the United States was the enemy of the Islamic world.

In America the amnesia came in various forms, the most intriguing evidence of which was furnished by President Carter during a press conference in February 1980. When asked about the American role in overthrowing the government of Iran in 1953, President Carter dismissed the question altogether by stating that it was "ancient history." What Carter refused to acknowledge was the strong link between the dilemma facing him and the history of American-Iranian relations. What Carter failed to tell the American public was that the eruption of simmering rage in Iran had much more to do with the oppressive policies of the Shah than with any blunders of his own administration. Especially remarkable was Carter's unwillingness or inability to explain to the American people that charges of mismanagement brought against him by his Republican opponents were at least equally applicable to the policies of his predecessors, particularly the Republican administrations that had dealt with the Shah of Iran.

President Carter's restraint or lack of political discernment—depending upon one's interpretation—went a long way to insure his election defeat in 1980. Carter's near silence in later years reinforced his role as the scapegoat of American politics and, for the second time in four years, prompted the Republican strategists to orchestrate a relentless campaign of misinformation against him. During the Republican Convention in 1984, Jimmy Carter was once again the target, and Walter Mondale—the man actually heading the Democratic ticket—was usually mentioned as an accomplice.

Of course, what made this phenomenon possible was that the American public came to associate Jimmy Carter with malaise and malfunctions of American foreign policy. More specifically, the American people were conditioned by the media to view Jimmy Carter's experience in Iran as that of a soft soldier who negotiated with savages while heroes were in captivity. Because the American people never appreciated soft soldiers, Jimmy Carter received a dishonorable discharge. This fascinating story, requiring the full cooperation of the American media and the Iranian militants, was created by promoting the sixty-four weeks of hostage hysteria and by pushing aside the ninety-seven years (1883–1979) of American-Iranian diplomatic history.

This study is an effort to break through the prevailing amnesia and to bring into focus, in light of new evidence and recent research, the story of the American experience in Iran. There have been, I will argue, two distinct historical periods in American involvement in Iran: the first beginning in 1911 with Morgan Shuster's mission as the financial advisor to the Iranian government and ending in 1954 with the imposition upon Iran of an Anglo-American oil agreement; the second covering the Shah's understandings with the United States government since 1954 and leading to the hostage hysteria of 1980. Differences between the two historical periods, I will argue, did not lie in the official attitude of the Iranian government but in the perceptions of the Iranian people. This study attempts to show that, since establishing diplomatic ties with the United States in 1883, the continual efforts of Persian authorities to invite American involvement in their country had the genuine support of the people of Iran, who had come to view the United States as something of a savior. But the benevolent image of America in Iran began to change in 1954, paving the way toward a critical and unflattering perception of America's role in that country and fostering a vast disparity between the pro-American stand of Persian authorities and the sentiments of the Iranian people.

To trace the transformation of America's image in Iran and to relate its relevance to the subsequent American experience, the primary focus of this inquiry has been the post–World War II era. I have reviewed the preceding period in two background chapters, in which I have addressed a number of factors relating to the central theme of this study. These include the role of Anglo-Russian imperial rivalry in Iran, the anticolonial posture of the United States, and the making of America's image as the savior of subjugated peoples. The background also includes a section that draws from archival data and presents a description of Iran during the Second World War, an assessment of the wartime propaganda campaign, and a review of the emergence of American interests in that country.

In examining the postwar American policies in Iran, the two most significant events—the Azerbaijan crisis of 1946 and the overthrow of Musaddiq in 1953, which led to the oil agreement of 1954—are selected and are given detailed analysis. These events, apart from being central to the study of American-Iranian relations, are excellent examples of different methods as well as different interpretations of America's strategy of containment. I have attempted to recount the details concerning each event within the context of America's global strategies. I have also attempted to examine the relations between ends and means by first considering each case as it was perceived by political actors at the time and then as it appears in historical perspective. In following this format, I have sought to deal with some lingering questions surrounding the Truman-Stalin confrontation in the Azerbaijan crisis, and to elucidate the nature and the extent of Eisenhower's responsibility in sowing the seeds of future trouble in Iran.

Truman's stand against Stalin in 1946, undoubtedly one of the most successful tests of the American strategy of containment, still conjures up debate concerning the method by which Truman compelled Stalin to remove the Red Army from Iran. Simply stated, the argument is over the authenticity of Truman's contention that he sent a threatening message to Stalin. In 1978, for example, one author sought to prove the nonexistence of a threatening message and accused the late president of a lack of candor and integrity. And in 1980, two others followed suit by claiming that Truman's account of the story was incorrect and that a threatening message was neither issued nor delivered to Stalin. But as shall be explained in detail, I have attempted to make it emphatically clear that inadequate research and the failure to consider the appropriate historical context account for such allegations.

Despite the publication of much literature in recent years, many features of American involvement in Iran during the 1950s have not been illuminated. An outstanding example of such features is the role of the American military strategy that was formulated as a back-up to the covert operation that toppled Musaddiq in 1953. Apparently, the military plan was such a well-kept secret that even Kermit Roosevelt, who was in charge of the covert operation, had no idea that, if the operation were to fail, the United States was contemplating direct military intervention in Iran. There is an effort in this study to shed some light on the origin, the specific course of action, and the significance of the military option.

Generally speaking, however, the principal obstacle to a systematic and comprehensive analysis of American policies in Iran during the 1950s has been the unavailability of complete historical records for the period. To be sure, a good deal of relevant information has thus far been declassified. But it is still incomplete, and to pretend otherwise is to mislead the students of history. In fact, I was informed by the staff of the National Archives that some of the records that were made available to me during 1980–82 were later reclassified. It may, of course, be argued that declassified documents already reveal most of the relevant facts. Nevertheless, ultimate confirmation becomes possible only if and when the complete records of the period are released. This is not to dismiss the valuable contribution of archival information but to acknowledge the limits of its availability and the need for future research.

To compensate for possible gaps in the diplomatic record, I secured interviews with some American and Iranian officials who participated in shaping American-Iranian relations during the 1950s. Although most individuals whom I interviewed requested anonymity, I am permitted to thank Mr. Paul Nitze for sharing his recollections and for furnishing me with his unpublished personal papers relating to Iran. I must also thank Mr. Kermit Roosevelt for a series of interviews during which he offered insightful and candid remarks. For their part, the Iranian officials were most helpful in explaining the factors that led to the rise of Dr. Musaddiq and the internal political divisions that contributed to his demise.

Finally, an account of American involvement in Iran in the 1960s and 1970s is presented in the epilogue of this study. It is an overview based on interviews, journalistic reports, and personal observations. I regard this approach as both necessary and honest. It is necessary because the archival records are not available and because I do not consider the documents captured and released by the Iranian militants as a reliable body of information. It is honest because, unlike some recent books on Iran, it does not pretend to do what is at present impossible—to tell the whole complicated story of American-Iranian relations.

During research for this study, which coincided with continuous antagonism between Tehran and Washington, I was often exposed to questions regarding my personal motives. Was I going to write an indictment of or an apology for American policies in Iran? It was a crowding sort of question, for it implied that my mind was already made up and that the merit of this work rested upon whose side it was on. Nevertheless, and despite being oversimplified, it was a legitimate question because it demanded to know the particular bias of this inquiry. Subsequently, I found myself confronting two basic options. The first was to follow the commonly used method of presenting a series of selected facts garnished with occasional and inconclusive commentary. The second option involved accepting the responsibility of clearly explaining my judgments as well as the criteria on which these judgments were based. Favoring the second option, I have put forward in the opening chapter an interpretive framework that deals with contrasting views of American-Soviet rivalry and their relation to the fate of Third World countries such as Iran. The intention is to provide an overview of topics that are essential to analysis of American strategies in the Third World and that help to delineate the frame of reference of this inquiry.

Far from describing this work as an "unbiased account of history"—in any event an illusory goal—I have merely sought to avoid romantic notions concerning the struggle of the Third World and the strategies of imperial powers. I am interested, not in the moral charms of subjugated peoples, but in their efforts to define their options and to overcome their predicament. I am concerned, not with the endless debates about the morality of imperialism, but with its efficacy and management.

Acknowledgments

I should like to express my thanks for the encouragement and support provided by Dean George Packard and by the faculty and the staff at the School of Advanced International Studies, The Johns Hopkins University. I am grateful to the late Professor Robert Osgood, whose integrity, intellectual tolerance, and guidance permitted me to produce this work. I feel especially indebted to Professor Frederick Holborn—undoubtedly one of the most unselfish and dedicated professors at SAIS—for reviewing the manuscript at various stages and for sharing his remarkable recollection of events and historical data. I also feel privileged for having the counsel of Professor Fouad Ajami, whose scholarly standards and insights have been a constant source of inspiration.

Professor Majid Khadduri, with his seasoned judgment and long scholarly experience, gave the manuscript a discerning critique. Professors Roger Savory, Waldo Heinrichs, Menahem Milson, and Arthur Goldschmidt read the manuscript and provided most helpful advice. Charles Appleby contributed much to this work through many hours of stimulating discussion. While working as a Research Associate at the Woodrow

Wilson International Center for Scholars, I had the opportunity to meet with a number of visiting scholars and benefit from their advice. I should like to thank Dr. James Billington and Dr. Samuel Wells for affording me this opportunity.

The kindnesses of Sally Marks and John Taylor of the National Archives, Peter Promen and Linda Carlson of SAIS library, Ibrahim Pourhadi and George Atiyeh of the Library of Congress are gratefully acknowledged. I extend my appreciation to Carolyn Law for typing the manuscript with outstanding skill and efficiency.

As a new author, I feel fortunate to have had the opportunity of working with the staff of the Pennsylvania State University Press. I owe a debt of gratitude to Chris Kentera, Director of the Press, for his expert guidance in preparing the manuscript for publication. I must also thank Ann Bates, a talented editor, for enthusiastic assistance throughout. And I think most authors would concede that a competent copy editor is an invaluable ally. This I fully realized after working with Kathleen Roos.

An article based on Chapter 4 of this manuscript and entitled "Truman Against Stalin in Iran: A Tale of Three Messages" appeared in the Winter 1987 issue of Middle Eastern Studies. *I am grateful for the permission to use the same material.*

Finally, I would like to express my deepest appreciation for my friends Martha Johns, G. W. Pasha, and Donna Lea Berg for their unfailing support and kindness.

Kuross A. Samii
Washington, D.C.
January 1987

1

American-Soviet Rivalry and the Third World: An Interpretive Framework

When weaving together the story of the past and judging the actions of political actors, the personal bias of individual authors plays a major role in creating various images of human behavior. This does not reduce the significance of scholarship but imposes an obligation upon scholars to clearly explain the interpretive framework through which they seek to assign meaning to historical events. To acquaint the reader with the frame of reference of this inquiry, this chapter deals with contrasting perceptions and interpretations of American-Soviet rivalry to provide an analytical context for addressing American policies toward Third World nations such as Iran. There is no pretense that the discussion of American-Soviet rivalry and the Third World viewpoint presented in this chapter can adequately deal with every aspect of these topics. The intention, however, is to provide an overview of the issues that help to explain the angry divide separating the major powers from each other and from Third World countries.

CONTRASTING PERCEPTIONS

At the historical roots of the United States' approach to international politics was a sense of mission shaped by eighteenth-century philosophy and Protestant evangelism advocating the universalism of American ideals.[1] Adherence to ideals (e.g., freedom and self-determination) was merged with a positive view of the nation's ability to shape history. America's sense of mission, however, was continuously tamed by an isolationist impulse that forbade entanglements in the affairs of the Old World. The American involvement in the First World War did not alter this pattern. Far from symbolizing the abandonment of isolationism, World War I became another test of America's resolve to confine her concerns to her own shores. President Wilson's preoccupation with creating a new international order proved disappointing to him and those American leaders who had envisioned a global role for the United States.

Against such historical tradition, the onset of the Second World War produced a revolutionary change in America's willingness to become involved with the destiny of other nations. This time, American participation went far beyond fighting the symptoms of the world malaise—World War II. It concentrated on the causes of such malaise—the social and economic ills of Europe. As early as January 6, 1941, almost a year before the attack on Pearl Harbor, Franklin D. Roosevelt, in his "Four Freedoms" speech, set the tone for America's postwar aims by proclaiming that "We will not accept a world like the post war world of the 1920's, in which the seeds of Hitlerism can again be planted and allowed to grow."[2] In a concerted effort to avoid the mistakes of the past, the American leaders were determined to disarm the defeated armies, promote America's ideal of self-determination, establish a new collective security organization, and rebuild the war-torn economies. This was a tall order, but it was deemed necessary if America was to win the war and the peace that would follow.

The destruction of the old international system, which had begun with the economic depression and the rise of fascism, ended with the defeat of Germany and Japan. Over the smoldering ashes of Europe and Japan rose the two great powers, the United States and the Soviet Union. With the rise of this bipolar structure of power, the United States began to associate security with maintenance of international order. The expanding peripheries of the international system became a battleground for the U.S.-U.S.S.R. struggle for security and influence. The interwar lesson concerning the dangers of piecemeal aggression fostered a similar fear regarding Communist penetration. This concern paved the way for the emergence of a rationale that placed any immediate Communist target within the broader context of the global confrontation between the United States and the Soviet Union.

Counterposed to the American view of the world were the perceptions of the other rising superpower, the Soviet Union. The traditional Russian sense of mission was based on the sixteenth-century idea of Moscow as a "Third Rome" and the nineteenth-century "pan-Slavic" movement, which foresaw a larger destiny for Russia than her frontiers.[3] After 1917, the ideological foundation furnished by Marxism-Leninism brought both clarity and confusion to the Soviet view of the world. The clarity was related to the acceptance of Marxism-Leninism, which predicted that all societies were destined to proceed along stages of development leading to socialist revolution and finally evolving into the classless society of Communism. Based upon the continuous class struggle, this view of human society considered the non-Communist states, particularly the capitalist countries, a threat to the Soviet Union.

Confronting external reality with the Marxian framework also brought confusion to the Soviet system. It is important to remember that Karl Marx and Friedrich Engels had spent the latter part of their lives thinking that socialist revolution was imminent in industrialized countries. Therefore, Lenin and his comrades were left with the challenge of explaining why the revolution had swept Russia instead of Germany or England. Similarly, Stalin had to deal with confusion regarding the idea of "World Revolution," which he was forced to abandon to concentrate on Russia's pressing internal problems.

On balance, however, ideology has been subordinated to Russia's self-interest. As demonstrated during the Second World War, Soviet leaders welcomed aid from anyone, including the capitalist states. The German invasion increased Russian fears of outside powers and compelled the Communist leaders to endorse the traditional Russian belief that security was directly linked to the amount of territory that Russia controlled. At the Tehran Conference, Stalin acknowledged that if the Soviet territory had not been so vast the Red Army would have been defeated.[4] The following statement by Stalin gives a clear indication of Soviet aims: "This war is not as in the past; whoever occupies territory also imposes on it his own social system. Everyone imposes his own system as far as his army can reach. It cannot be otherwise."[5]

The conduct of Soviet officials in the occupied territories also indicated that Stalin had every intention of either annexing such territories or controlling them by inserting puppet regimes loyal to Moscow. In the case of Iran, a massive Soviet propaganda campaign was designed to convince the Persians that their future was linked with the Soviet Union and that the Russians would remain after the war to rebuild Iran.[6] Soviet goals were no less ambitious with regard to other occupied countries. As the immediate postwar history demonstrates, whereas the Soviets were successful in implementing their plans in Eastern Europe, they failed elsewhere because of the pressure exerted by the United States.

Declassified documents establish beyond reasonable doubt that the United States government was aware of Soviet motives in the early stages of the Second World War.[7] This fact is also supported in Thomas Powers's splendid book *The Man Who Kept the Secrets*. The author traces the career of Richard Helms by combing through the history of the Office of Strategic Services (OSS) and the Central Intelligence Agency (CIA). "The long debate over the origins of the Cold War would strike OSS veterans later as a silly exercise," writes Powers. "In their experience the Cold War was a corollary of the shooting war from the beginning."[8] As early as the battle of Stalingrad, it was reported that Allen Dulles, the OSS's chief of mission in Bern, Switzerland, was beginning to shift his attention from Germany to Russia. Other OSS officers, including Richard Helms, came to accept the Soviet-American rivalry as a fact throughout the war. In short, the Cold War had begun long before it was named.[9]

In the face of evidence that clearly indicates American awareness of the Soviet antagonism, why was FDR's public posture so different from his private convictions? The best answer was given by FDR himself: "My children, it is permitted you in time of grave danger to walk with the devil until you have crossed the bridge."[10] Beyond the exigencies of the war, Roosevelt's tolerance of Stalin was necessitated by postwar American plans. Since the broad security interests of the United States were identified with the viability of a new international order, cooperation with the Soviet Union was required. For the long run, there was hope that Russia's internal problems would burst the Communist bubble and thus make Russia more amenable to cooperation with the United States.

For the Russians, the specter of Americans replacing the British as their chief imperial rival was disquieting, but the need for American military assistance dictated tolerance toward the United States. For their part, the Soviets were hoping that in the long run the capitalist societies would self-destruct. The Marxian script had already described this eventuality. More significant, there was an assumption that the behavior of the capitalist societies was as predictable as in Lenin's dictum: "Fully aware that it would be used to hang him, a capitalist still can not resist the profit from selling the rope." The assumption that the capitalists were predictable did play a major role in modifying the Soviet fear of cooperation with the United States.

As the policy of mutual tolerance continued, a variety of factors—conditioned by the clash of the Russian concept of security and the American ideal of self-determination, manifested in Eastern Europe, Germany, Iran, and elsewhere—began to cause the disintegration of the Grand Alliance. What began as FDR's disenchantment with Stalin eventually evolved into the Truman Doctrine and open hostility with the Soviet Union, which in essence divided the globe into spheres of domination. In retrospect, it appears that, beyond the goal of defeating their common enemies, there was little reason for the U.S.-Soviet cooperation, except for the possibility of deciding their domains without yielding to the vulgarities of Cold War rhetoric.

CONTRASTING INTERPRETATIONS

The degree of American and Soviet responsibility in commencing and continuing the Cold War has been the subject of continual debate. Beyond the diversity in the intellectual orientation of scholars, the differences in interpretation are associated with varying perceptions of the period in which the Cold War originated. Those who are inclined to attribute the Cold War to ideology usually find its origins in the Russian Revolution of 1917. For example, Andre Fontaine, in *History of the Cold War,* finds the roots of Soviet aggressiveness in the Communist ideology. But James Nathan and James Oliver, while recognizing Soviet antagonism, have found the "Wilsonian vision" a significant contributor to the American-Soviet hostility. They write:

But the expansive Wilsonian values of the world order based on a comprehensive political capitalism had already contributed much to what would come to be the Cold War. Wilsonian policy was a precursor of the ideologically motivated decisions of later years and later administrations and, as such, forms the opening phrases of the dialogue of distrust that characterize the Cold War.[11]

In offering a somewhat different view, Arnold Toynbee contends that America's reaction to Communism has been a symptom of a dramatic reversal of America's historic role as the revolutionary leader of the depressed majority of mankind. Since 1917, America has become the archconservative power by discarding her revolutionary role of the past and presenting it to her archenemy, the Soviet Union.[12]

Some students of the Cold War have found its origins in the events of World War II. In *A History of the Cold War*, John Lukacs considers the meeting of Russian and American troops along the Elbe on April 25, 1945, a "symbolic event." This event, which led to the division of Germany and most of Europe into American and Soviet spheres of influence, "marks the supreme condition of contemporary history. . . . The so-called Cold War grew out of this division."[13] For Vojtech Mastny, *Russia's Road to the Cold War* was paved by Hitler's attack on Russia, which provided the dubious justification for Stalin's imperialism. The enduring memory of a narrow escape from defeat fostered a pervasive militarism in the Soviet Union. Professor Mastny suggests that, considering Russia's condition at the end of World War II, Western policy should have followed a harder line. The failure of the Western leaders to impress upon Stalin the limits of their tolerance produced the East-West confrontation.[14]

The tension between the American ideal of self-determination and the Soviet concern for security is depicted by John Lewis Gaddis as the cause of the disintegration of the Grand Alliance.[15] The conferences of Tehran and Yalta, failing to reconcile the differences, produced an ambiguity by which each side could interpret the agreements in accordance with its own special interests. By the end of the war, however, the differences could no longer be ignored. The subsequent hard-line policy of President Truman produced another debate among historians regarding whether or not Truman caused an immediate reversal of FDR's policies. Authors of diverse intellectual leanings are found on the same side of this debate. For example, those accounts that have stressed the continuity of policy include Gabriel Kolko's *Politics of War: The World and the United States* and John Lewis Gaddis's *United States and the Origins of the Cold War.* Accounts that have suggested a reversal of policy by Truman include Gar Alperovitz's *Atomic Diplomacy: Hiroshima and Potsdam,* Elliott Roosevelt's *As He Saw It,* and D. F. Fleming's *Cold War and Its Origins, 1917–1950.*

A more fundamental dividing line among historians was created by the degree of their acceptance or rejection of the official point of view. The official or orthodox view of the Cold War was put forward by American and British leaders in speeches and in personal and official documents. As explained by Arthur Schlesinger, Jr., the orthodox view states that the Cold War was the brave and essential response of free men to Communist aggression.[16] The historians of the 1950s generally accepted the official explanations, although some expressed reservations regarding specific policies. Among writers who accepted a more limited version of the official interpretations, one can find Walter Lippmann, Hans Morgenthau, and George Kennan. The latter made it clear in his *Memoirs 1925–1950* that he did not approve of the intensity of the American response to the perceived Soviet challenge. The disagreement among those who rejected one or more aspects of the official interpretation—as pointed out by Norman Graebner—is not over the nature or the morality of the Soviet behavior but over its meaning. For example, Walter Lippmann, while recognizing the existence of a Russian problem, accepted the notion that a Soviet sphere of influence was a logical expression of the times and not necessarily a danger to the West.[17]

During the 1960s a group of scholars who were labeled revisionists began to receive attention. Rejection of the orthodox view was the principal proposition of this school of thought. The degree of dismissal of the official explanation, and the intellectual orientation from which they criticized the American policies, in turn subdivided the revisionists. In *The Radical Left and American Foreign Policy,* Robert W. Tucker has identified two broad categories of critics. The first are referred to as the liberal-realist critics, who have argued that America entered the post–World War II period without a clear and consistent view of her role in the world. They suggest that this confusion led to the gradual universalization of the Truman Doctrine, which resulted in an overcommitment of America's resources. Their central theme proposes that failures of American diplomacy are related to sentimentality and intellectual errors, leading to tragedies such as Vietnam.[18]

Another group of revisionists, what Professor Tucker has called the "Radical Left," finds little confusion or uncertainty. Unlike the liberal-realists, who have often questioned the competence of American leaders, the radical critics have generally depicted American leaders as quite competent in serving American corporate interests. The aim of American diplomacy is rather clear in that it is formulated solely to serve American capitalism. Since the old colonial method of exploitation was deemed inefficient, the "open door" policy was inaugurated to secure America's access to desirable world markets. The Wilsonian vision of seeking a new international system is described as another scheme to promote a pro-American equilibrium to safeguard America's preponderant economic power.[19]

Radical historiography further suggests that the course of American diplomacy during and following the Second World War was in essence a more aggressive Wilsonian version of a stable world order under the leadership of American capitalism.[20] For example, Walter Lafeber has argued that U.S. aggressiveness toward the Soviet Union was the result of pressing the "open door" policy. While American plans succeeded in Western Europe, they failed in Eastern Europe.[21] Similarly, Gabriel Kolko contends that the conflict with the Soviet Union was the result of a strategy intent upon establishing an integrated world capitalist order under American control.[22]

The radical critique dismisses the American security concern on the ground that the vast American superiority at the end of the Second World War should have ruled out such anxieties.[23] Instead, it is vehement in demonstrating that America misused her power. The charges that America has become the greatest threat to world peace were registered by Noam Chomsky. Another indictment, by Carl Oglesby, went even further by calling America "history's most violent nation."[24] It should be pointed out, however, that charges of misuse of power by the United States are not confined to the radical critique. For example, in *Atomic Diplomacy: Hiroshima and Potsdam*, Gar Alperovitz has argued that Truman delayed the Potsdam Conference in order to break the news of the bomb. Then, having failed to impress Stalin at Potsdam, Truman used the bomb against Japan, not to end the war—since he already knew of Japan's willingness to surrender—but to provide an actual demonstration of American power for Stalin.[25]

In brief, the revisionism of the radical historiography is distinctive, not because it considers America aggressive and imperialistic, and not because it suggests that America misused her power to create the confrontation with the Soviet Union, but because it contends that American actions were necessitated by the institutional needs of American capitalism.[26]

Generally speaking, the strengths and weaknesses of the radical critique have not been adequately explicated in the literature. Whereas its proponents have often failed to present a concise argument, its overzealous opponents have focused on some relatively insignificant issues while totally overlooking the fundamental flaws that accompany the logic of the radical critique. But then, this is precisely why the work of Professor Tucker deserves special attention, for it addresses the essential arguments of the radical critique and provides an insightful and fair evaluation.

When listing the merits of the radical historiography, Tucker points to its success in demonstrating the extent to which an obsessive self-interest has been present in American foreign policy, and thus in providing a degree of realism that often has been missing from the conventional historiography. "Even in exaggeration," Tucker writes, "the radical emphasis seems nearer the truth than liberal-realist historiography." In fact, Tucker concedes that the radical critique is much nearer to the truth than his own earlier declaration that "America is perhaps history's example par excellence of a state that reluctantly, and apologetically, acquired imperial power."[27]

The radical historiography also corrects some misconceptions regarding America's involvement in world affairs. To explain America's interventionist policies in terms of ideological obsession is not only incorrect, but, as Tucker concedes, it gives American policies a quality of innocence that they do not possess. American policies cannot be adequately explained in terms of an abstract ideological commitment that is divorced from interest and oblivious to political realities.[28] Another needed correction of the conventional historiography relates to the contention that the one theme indispensable to an understanding of the Cold War is the disparity between the universalist and sphere-of-influence views. Arthur Schlesinger, Jr., has suggested that America was the champion of the universalist view, which sought security through international organization, and that the Soviet Union adhered to the sphere-of-influence concept and thus sought security by the balance of power.[29] But here again, Tucker is in agreement with the radical critique that the description of American policies as universalist and opposed to the sphere-of-influence concept is not correct. To begin with, the United States had a continued claim to a sphere of influence in the Western Hemisphere. America never seriously relied upon multilateralism to safeguard her vital interests, and her adherence to the United Nations Charter by no means indicated the complete abandonment of America's unilateralism. In fact, the United Nations Charter was deliberately set up so as to grant the great powers complete freedom of action. The United States' support of the collective security system was at best a hope that this organization might be of some assistance in consolidating America's leadership in the postwar period. America's universalism simply indicated that America was opposed to certain kinds of spheres of influence, precisely the kind that the Soviet Union had in mind in Eastern Europe.[30]

The radical critique, however, goes one step further by insisting that America wanted to make the entire world an American sphere of domination. "If the radical response is overdrawn, if it fails to acknowledge the security motive that entered into American policy," Tucker observes, "it nevertheless contains a core of truth. Yet it is only by juxtaposition with an orthodox historiography that this response appears startling."[31]

Despite his recognition of the merits of the radical critique, Tucker's rejection of this school of thought is complete and clearly expressed. Tucker, wisely, does not waste the space to argue against the fact that America has been an imperial power, that America has pursued self-interest vigorously, and that America has been interventionist and antirevolutionary. Instead, Tucker confronts the radical critique in the following fashion:

> America's interventionist and counterrevolutionary policy is the expected response of an imperial power with a vital interest in maintaining an order that, apart from the material benefits this order confers, has become synonymous with the nation's vision of its role in history. Yet this vision cannot be understood in ideological terms alone. In the manner of all imperial visions, it is also solidly rooted in the will to exercise dominion over others.... [32]

Furthermore, Tucker refutes the radical critique's assertion that America's behavior is rooted in the institutions of American capitalism.

Tucker contends that American conduct has more to do with American power than with the requirements of American capitalism. In pursuing this line of reasoning, he asks, "Why may we not say simply that the interests of states expand roughly with their power and that America has been no exception to this experience?"[33] He further contends that "the method of indirect and informal empire is not an American invention. It is not even a capitalist invention."[34]

Finally, in dismissing the radical historiography's principal argument, that the history of American diplomacy is only explainable by the history of American capitalism, Tucker observes that it is power itself, more than a particular form of power, that prompts expansion. He concludes: "Thus the radical criticism will not confront the eternal and insoluble problems inordinate power creates, just as it will not acknowledge that men possessed of this power are always ready to use it if only in order to rule over others."[35]

On balance, however, it appears that it is not the radical critique that suffers the most under Tucker's scrutiny. Despite Tucker's rejection of the radical critique's argument that capitalism explains America's behavior, a major portion of this critique remains remarkably intact. Its allegation that America has behaved aggressively in pursuit of an obsessive self-interest is not seriously challenged, and certainly not discredited. What are most discredited by Tucker's analysis are the conventional historiography and the so-called liberal-realist critics, who have attributed American behavior to sentimentality and intellectual errors. Whereas the radical critique is credited with bringing a degree of realism into the discussion of American foreign policy, the liberal-realist historiography is stripped of the very element upon which it has prided itself—its realism.

Although Tucker's analysis is essentially correct, his tendency to depict the various critics as having the same view is indeed questionable. For example, Tucker suggests that the differences between William A. Williams, the idealist, and Gabriel Kolko, the economic determinist, are not significant, because if their arguments are pushed to a logical conclusion, the result is an indictment of American institutions. As Tucker puts it, "Williams' necessity may be a psychic necessity but his psychic necessity is still, at bottom, an institutional necessity."[36]

Contrary to Tucker's argument, however, a fundamental difference is still present. Above all, Williams reveals a sense of indignation and frustration at what he considers to be the perversion of American ideals. If Williams attacks American institutions, he is presumably seeking a reconstruction of such institutions that would be nearer to the nation's ideals. By contrast, Kolko considers American ideals as empty rhetoric that is useless for reconstruction of any institution. It may, of course, be argued that Williams suffers from an intellectual error because his perception of American ideals is too romantic and thus impractical and incorrect. Only in this vein can it be suggested that Williams and Kolko have similar views because both are advocating an institutional change based on values alien to American ideals.

The contrast between Kolko and Williams is also reminiscent of the contrast between two groups of critics who have attacked Soviet institutions. There are many writers who revel in condemning Soviet institutions in the same manner that Kolko has indicted American institutions—by contending that moral values have been disregarded. They have concluded that everything concerning Marxism is evil and that the Russian leaders are prisoners of Marxian ideology and Soviet bureaucracy. In contrast to this view, there are those whose objection to Soviet conduct is reminiscent of Williams's objection to American behavior—by contending that ideology has been misinterpreted. An outstanding example of such writers is Michael Harrington. In *Socialism,* he emphasizes the humanitarian and democratic bases of original Marxism and assails Lenin for using Marxism to justify his own dictatorship.[37]

A salient assumption, however, is implied by both Williams and Harrington. The very suggestion that ideology has been misinterpreted assumes the freedom of choice for those who interpreted ideologies and designed policies. By contrast, Kolko, who has depicted the American leaders as the puppets of capitalism, and others, who have described the Soviet leaders as the prisoners of Communism, have denied this freedom. Such denial not only removes the question of the historical responsibility of American and Soviet leaders but portrays them as pathetic pawns and, in the final analysis, deprives them of their final dignity, that of being a man.

The foregoing discussion, while containing a rainbow of interpretations, has little to say about a prescription for future policies. This is not to suggest that such prescriptions do not exist, but that the debate over past policies has been colorful enough to overshadow ideas regarding a future course of action. Among the scholars who have been able to look beyond the immediate debate and provide clearly stated prescriptions are Professors Tucker and Williams. In defending the desirability of an imperial America, Tucker advocates the use of all available means to preserve America's preponderant economic and military power. In Tucker's words:

> The abandonment of an interventionist policy will improve the chances for the emergence to power in the developing nations of regimes that are, if not Communist, at least strongly nationalist and collectivist in character. That these regimes will act independently and in terms of their own interests does not mean that their interests will prove congenial to American interests. However complete their independence of action, their very existence will reduce America's influence and thereby threaten the larger interest with which America has come to identify its integrity and well-being.[38]

Counterposed to Tucker's view is the judgment of Professor Williams that America's behavior is reprehensible and that "preserving the empire is an exercise in futility." Williams contends that American history has raised the following questions: "Is the idea and reality of America possible without empire? Can you even imagine America as not an empire?" Williams's own conclusion is that "once we imagine it, break out of the imperial idiom, we just might be able to create a nonimperial America."[39]

As diametrically opposed as the opinions of Professors Tucker and Williams may appear, they have an essential element in common—the courage to acknowledge the reality of American empire. Tucker's concern with America's supremacy within the Hobbesian nature of international affairs, and Williams's call for America's leadership to alter such sordid affairs, are both genuine and derive from a willingness to confront the uncomfortable evidence. This willingness underscores the strength of their approach to the study of history and separates both scholars from those who have either ignored the reality of American or Soviet empires or have sought to equate empires with global justice and liberty.

Finally, the seemingly endless debates of the 1960s and 1970s are now beginning to bear fruit. On April 8, 1983, John Lewis Gaddis went before the Organization of American Historians to formally announce the acceptance of the idea that America has been an imperial power, and that recognizing the existence of American-Soviet imperial rivalry should be the point of departure for any serious analysis of American or Soviet strategies. From the clashes of the old orthodoxy and revisionism, Gaddis declared, a new synthesis was emerging, which he called "postrevisionism." According to Gaddis, while postrevisionism acknowledges America's imperial role, it does maintain that the Americans, unlike the Russians, have not always attempted to impose their will upon other countries.[40]

In celebrating the birth of postrevisionism, Gaddis reported other important trends. These included a rising interest in archival data to test the old assumptions regarding the nature of American strategy, and an emphasis upon studies that provide concrete examples of American behavior in various regions and countries. Moreover, Gaddis claimed that historians were adopting a mature attitude that promises to reduce the petty and sterile arguments of the past. As Gaddis put it, "We have at last begun, so to speak, to 'put away childish things.' "[41]

If the so-called postrevisionism assumes the prominent role that Gaddis hopes it does, the study of American foreign policy will receive a healthy dose of realism. The debate may then center on the efficacy of American empire rather than on its existence. This in itself will be a triumph of common sense over the traditional fear of acknowledging America's imperial role. Furthermore, if the new trends that Gaddis spoke of are here to stay, the quality of future literature should certainly improve. Instead of relying upon labels such as "Marxist," "fascist," "terrorist," and "freedom fighters" to explain away complex social movements, historians and policymakers alike may be compelled more than ever before to investigate the nature of such movements and to learn of the possible consequences for the future of American foreign policy.

THIRD WORLD VIEWPOINT

Intimately associated with the analysis of American foreign policy, particularly American-Soviet rivalry, is the viewpoint of the so-called Third World countries. It may be stated at the outset that the phrase "Third World viewpoint" is simply a shorthand for denoting some opinions shared by people from diverse intellectual orientations. In essence, the Third World perspective refers to a variety of political beliefs that are linked by a common denominator that indicts the imperial policies of major powers and is concerned with the impact of American-Soviet rivalry on the rest of the world.[42]

A substantial degree of confusion, nevertheless, surrounds the Third World perspective, some of which is attributable to authors who have incorrectly characterized this viewpoint. An example of such authors is Charles Maier. Commenting on revisionism, Maier writes, "Above all, they [revisionists] approach history with a value system and a vocabulary that appear to make meaningful historical dialogue with those who do not share their framework impossible."[43] Ironically, in the same article, Maier approaches the Third World viewpoint with a value system and a vocabulary that appear to make any dialogue with those who do not share *his* framework impossible.

To begin with, Maier imparts the impression that he is addressing one specific Third World perspective by describing his target as "a 'third world' viewpoint which can indict both major world powers and supply a 'usable past' for those morally overwhelmed by an updated Holy Alliance between Moscow and Washington."[44] This description, far from designating any specific Third World viewpoint, merely indicates the common denominators contained in all variations of Third World perspectives. It is in conjunction with such a general description, however, that Maier puts forward his criticism of the Third World perspective:

> Attractive though it may be in the light of current events, this third world perspective has serious analytical deficiencies. First of all, its Marxian basis imposes an overly schematic view of motivation; it precludes any possibility that American policy makers might have acted from genuine emancipatory impulses or even in uncertainty. . . . [45]

First of all, to characterize the basis of the Third World viewpoint as necessarily Marxian is simply irresponsible because a wide range of intellectual orientations is affiliated with this viewpoint. As a political guide, it is associated with the so-called nonaligned movement, which comprises democracies, dictatorships, authoritarian and totalitarian regimes. It includes socialists as well as Islamic fundamentalists. That some Marxists—who oppose Soviet imperialism as vigorously as they oppose American imperialism—have supported the Third World viewpoint does not necessarily make it Marxian. It may still come as a revelation to some that one need not be a Marxist to recognize American imperialism, nor is it necessary to be a non-Marxist to notice Soviet imperialism.

Second, to suggest that the Third World viewpoint "precludes any possibility" of perceiving altruism or uncertainty in the conduct of the United States is not only unwarranted but creates unnecessary confusion. Whether or not American or Soviet actions may have been inspired at times by magnanimity or by mistake has little to do with the principal argument that both superpowers have generally acted in the manner of all imperial powers. What is being sidestepped by Charles Maier are the following questions: Does the kindness of a master toward a servant alter their fundamental relationship? Does the American or the Soviet philanthropic impulse indicate that they are willing to cease exercising their power to dominate others? Does it change the fundamental problem that men possessed of power are willing to use it to rule over others?

A disinclination to accept an affirmative answer for any of these questions is rooted in history. More recently, it is rooted in the conduct of present major powers, which have generally acted like the empires of the past. As before, the pervasive desire of powerful nations to expand and to protect their spheres of domination by the use or threat of force has remained unchanged.

To expose the inaccuracy of statements made by Charles Maier is not to suggest that the Third World viewpoint is free from serious flaws, but to propose that such flaws are revealed, not through attacking Marxism, but through a proper evaluation of the Third World viewpoint that recognizes both its strengths and its weaknesses and that rationally delineates its fragility.

Essentially, what gives strength to the Third World perspective is the legitimacy of the basic assertion that power in the hands of the powerful has generally been used to dominate the weak. Based upon this assertion, the grievances of Third World societies were articulated in the historic meeting of nonaligned countries in Bandung in 1955. These grievances had a long history that predated the emergence of American-Soviet rivalry. Nevertheless, the charges of hypocrisy and misdeeds made against both the United States and the Soviet Union became the core of the Third World explanation of global economic and political injustice.

The charges of misdeeds made against the United States are often juxtaposed with professed American ideals. Whereas the American ideals of freedom and self-determination stand in opposition to America's involvement in overthrowing the governments of other sovereign countries, they have not prevented the United States government from participating in such acts. Whereas American ideals cast an unfavorable shadow upon dictatorships, they have not prevented the United States government from courting such regimes. America's support for dictators and ruling families who do not represent anything above and beyond themselves is portrayed by the Third World perspective as indicating that the maximization of America's economic and military interests has generally been the guiding light of the United States' foreign relations.

The portrayal of America as an imperial and antirevolutionary force, however, is hardly confined to Marxists or to some deranged habitual haters of the United States. For example, a decade before the full extent of the Vietnam tragedy was publicized, Arnold Toynbee observed:

> Today America is no longer the inspirer and leader of the World Revolution, and I have an impression that she is embarrassed and annoyed when she is reminded that this was her original mission. No one else laid this mission upon America. She chose it for herself, and for one hundred and forty-two years, reckoning from the year 1775, she pursued this revolutionary mission with an enthusiasm which has proved deservedly infectious. By contrast, America is today the leader of a world-wide anti-revolutionary movement in defence of vested interests. She now stands for what Rome stood for.... [46]

"What has happened?" wondered Toynbee. "[The] simplest account of it is, I suppose, that America has joined the minority. In 1775 she was in the ranks of the majority, and this is one reason why the American Revolution evoked a world-wide response."[47] The enthusiasm and the confidence that accompanied revolutionary America were transformed into dismay and distrust because the perception of America's role was changed. In Toynbee's words: "Lafayette pays a high psychological price when he transforms himself into Metternich. Playing Metternich is not a happy role. It is not a hero's role, and not a winner's role, and the player knows it."[48]

America's archrival, the Soviet Union, has not fared much better in the eyes of the Third World. As appealing as the egalitarian notion of Communism may be, Karl Marx pays a high psychological price when his ideas are transformed by the Soviet leaders. That is why the Third

World perspective could and does argue against placing a premium upon Marxism to explain Soviet behavior, for although Soviet Communism has brought new methods to the traditional Russian imperial designs, it has not modified the all-consuming pursuit of Russia's self-interest. Since 1917, Soviet assistance to revolutionary movements has been extended only when it has coincided with Russia's imperial interests. In fact, Soviet ideological commitments are reduced to empty rhetoric when they are weighed against the Soviet betrayal of revolutionary movements. As was the case with Stalin's betrayal of the ideological brethren in Greece, the Soviet Union has continuously exploited the romantic notions of socialism held by the youth of the Third World and then abandoned them as they became expendable. From all historical indications, it appears that the best guide to understanding Russia's behavior is not the writings of Marx but the works of Machiavelli.

Above all, the Third World perspective regards the ideological antagonism between Washington and Moscow as a fraud that allows the major powers to mobilize internal support for external aggression. The record of American and Soviet conduct generally indicates that both major powers have been willing to cooperate with anyone, including each other, as long as the cooperation results in economic and military gains or reduced inefficiencies and losses. Furthermore, the American, Soviet, and Chinese triangle is perceived as making a mockery of the ideological antagonism between capitalism and Communism. Whereas American leaders have depicted the Soviet Union as the "evil empire," American companies continue to do business with the Russians and to provide the Soviet Union with grains to feed the Red Army, enabling them to maintain a police state at home and to invade smaller countries. While the American government has continuously claimed to pursue an anti-Communist crusade, American leaders have traveled to Peking to embrace the Chinese Communists. Whatever the logic of American behavior, the result has been an erosion of American prestige in the Third World.

Of course, no less revealing is the behavior of the Communist powers. While enthusiastically courting the bosses of American capitalism, the Chinese have accused the Soviets of "ideological impurity." And the Soviets have been eager to do business with what they call "American imperialists" and acquire technology from the United States, a country that is referred to by Soviet leaders as the "warped society." While benefiting from trade with the West, the Soviet Union has methodically created a ring of terror that continuously consumes weaker states. Thus, in the eyes of the Third World, American-Soviet cooperation has helped the Soviet Union to solidify a state of affairs that bears a marked resemblance to an ever-expanding concentration camp.

Finally, the Third World perspective regards the selective application of so-called international law as a fig leaf intended to cover the behavior of powerful states. Both the United States and the Soviet Union are accused of making the United Nations the political circus of the world. Although much of the political clowning is often provided by the Third World countries, it is suggested that these countries merely perform there and are not responsible for the logic that created the rules of the game. The rationale that granted veto power to a few nations preserved the right of unilateral action for the powerful and thus paved the way for making the United Nations the laughingstock of world politics. There is no reason to believe, the argument goes, that any collectivity would respect regulations that may be vetoed by the powerful but imposed against the weak.

AN APPRAISAL

Overall, if the allegations that may be put forward by the Third World perspective appear overdrawn, if it tends to overlook the legitimate American or Soviet security concerns, it nevertheless contains a core of truth. This truth cannot be masked by labeling the Third World viewpoint as Marxist, nor can it be concealed by accusing it of being totally ungrateful for sincere American or Soviet gestures. On the contrary, such silly suggestions obscure the irresoluble irony inherent in the logic that accompanies the Third World perspective.

Implicit in the Third World argument is the suggestion that the United States and the Soviet Union are indicted, not because they are capitalist or Communist, but because they are accused of having exploited other nations. This amounts to admitting that the aggressive behavior of the two countries is explainable, not by the peculiarities of their ideologies, but by the similarities of their relative power. Thus, in the final analysis, the Third World perspective concedes that it is power itself, rather than any particular ideology, that feeds the desire to dominate others.

That power is the real arbiter of international relations, that it explains American or Soviet behavior above and beyond capitalism or Communism, quite inevitably exposes the vulnerability of Third World arguments. Indeed, if power is the element that dictates international relations, then there are no persuasive grounds for assuming that once a weak nation acquires power her behavior would be different from that of other powerful states. In fact, history clearly indicates that as nation-states began to emerge and accumulate power they followed the general behavior of all powerful states by attempting to dominate the weak. The newly powerful are even willing at times to collaborate with their previous colonial masters to exploit the cluster of countries left behind.

The conduct of the Third World countries also imparts no confidence that a change in the pattern of human behavior is about to emerge. If anything, the actions of the Third World governments generally demonstrate that their capacity for injustice by far exceeds that of the major powers whom they are accusing of injustice. As is often the case, improvement in the lot of the Third World countries becomes the tool of their leadership for eliminating political opposition more effectively, for inflicting pain upon weaker states, for paying off foreign journalists to forge a favorable image abroad, and for arranging vacations, or what are commonly referred to as "fact-finding missions," for the representatives of the major powers.

Militarily insignificant countries of the Third World, as might be expected, are easily overwhelmed by a perceived incremental rise of their power vis-à-vis their neighbors. The delusion of power is commonly created because of a civil war or change of leadership in a neighboring state. Predatory impulses are immediately at work to incite attacks against a vulnerable neighbor. To add insult to injury, ancient border disputes are customarily presented to the world as the cause of the invasion. What lends an air of black humor to such cases is that the leaders of aggressor states still regard themselves as the champions of the Third World crusade and often insist on hosting the Nonaligned Conference, which presumably coordinates the Third World struggle against the imperial powers.

Similarly, improvements in the finances of the Third World countries often act as a segregating factor within as well as among these nations. For example, despite the appearance to the contrary, the inflow of oil revenue to OPEC countries has accentuated the gap between rich and poor within these societies and has forged an alliance between the privileged classes of such countries and the financial institutions of the West, where they have buried their bounties. Furthermore, the newly rich of the Third World, while conveniently ignoring their own immediate past, have generally regarded the poor countries as some form of parasite. The bulk of the so-called foreign aid, particularly that given by the weak but oil-rich states of the Persian Gulf, has been primarily designed to pay off the troublemakers of the region who may threaten the imposed serenity of such countries. What is then fraudulently celebrated as a sign of generosity is in fact a protection fee.

The charges of hypocrisy and misdeeds made against the major powers, as the essence of Third World grievances, certainly lose their potency when juxtaposed with the conduct of most Third World governments. While slaughtering their citizens because of "infidelity" to the regime, Third World leaders have expressed concern for human rights elsewhere. While suffocating half of their population—women—by some convenient religious or social customs, they have objected to the treatment of blacks in America or minorities in Russia. While denying civil liberties to their citizens, they have dispatched delegations to international conferences to deplore the actions of others. The frequency of such behavior is what portrays the grievances of the Third World as the fraud of its mediocre leadership. And it is the pervasiveness of such traits that disputes the sincerity of Third World sermons and displays its utterances as an outcry for power and not an outrage against injustice.

In Third World countries where the past is deep, self-deception has become ingrained in the political culture. To overcome the despair of their predicament, the distant past is usually glorified, the recent past is often deplored, future salvation is always promised, and, above all, the present malaise is blamed on foreign powers. As is often the case, while seeking a powerful patron, the governments of the Third World have exaggerated the misdeeds of major powers to provide justification for the dictatorship without which they do not know how to rule, for the sacrifices they are bound to demand, and for the cruelties they dare not *not* to inflict. It is against this tired tradition that the facts and fictions of Third World grievances should be sorted out and placed in historical perspective.

CONCLUSIONS

The antagonism between powerful and powerless and between rich and poor nations, though largely emanating from their very predicament, is also related to their mutual misunderstandings and misconceptions. Compared to the American experience, the problem of misunderstanding has been less pronounced in Soviet relations with the Third World. The reason is, of course, that the Third World societies have learned from experience what to expect from the Soviet Union, and the Soviet leadership has done precious little to produce pleasant surprises. In brief, while Third World antagonism toward the Soviet Union is no less intense than that directed against the United States, the bitterness that usually accompanies a feeling of betrayal is often absent from Third World complaints against the Soviet Union.

The story of American relations with the Third World, however, reveals a good deal of mutual misconceptions and misunderstandings. An interesting account of American attitudes is contained in Robert Packenham's *Liberal America and the Third World*. "With respect strictly to Third World political development," writes Packenham, "the most severe intellectual 'hang up' of American officialdom and public opinion, if not also of its academic community, is not an excessively dogmatic Marxism but an excessively dogmatic liberal tradition. These ideas remain today, and will doubtless remain for some time to come, the most profound ideological contributors to American misconceptions about political development in poor countries." According to Packenham, while liberal constitutionalism is appropriate for the United States, its export to the Third World is inappropriate because of the absence of conditions necessary for political democracy.[49]

A similar view has been expressed by Professor Jeane Kirkpatrick. "Although most governments in the world are, as they always have been, autocracies of one kind or another," Kirkpatrick argues, "no idea holds greater sway in the mind of educated Americans than the belief that it is possible to democratize governments, anytime, anywhere, under any circumstances." In refuting the viability of this belief, Professor Kirkpatrick warns of the dangers it poses to American interests abroad. For example, she suggests that the Carter administration actively participated in toppling the Shah of Iran and Somoza of Nicaragua because of the mistaken assumptions that a democratic alternative could be imposed upon such societies and that the change in such autocracies was inevitable, desirable, and in the American interest.[50]

If exporting liberal democracy has indeed been a primary purpose of American foreign policy, then Professors Packenham and Kirkpatrick are absolutely correct in suggesting that this approach would lead to unfortunate results. The good intentions of American officials notwithstanding, such an approach conveys an intellectual arrogance and tends to overlook the fact that nations are separated by more than geographical boundaries and that cultural peculiarities have more to say about systems of government than an assumed universal set of ideals. The approach of American officials would thus bear the mark of Niebuhrian irony—of intentions that lead inexorably to contrary results because of errors of analysis and prescription.

The attitude of Third World societies also reveals a profound misconception of the West. Because of their own past experience, the people of the Third World tend to view the actions of any government, including those of Western democracies, as reflecting the conspiracy of the elite rather than the consensus of the general public. As a result, most Third World crusaders have been inclined to believe that they may acquire the support of public opinion in the West by publicizing the alleged misdeeds of Western governments. No elaborate inquest is necessary, however, to understand the disparity between such expectations and political reality. The following brief statement by Professor Tucker accurately explains the reason:

> If advanced states, whether Capitalist or Socialist, may behave similarly in many respects toward backward states, it is not simply because they are advanced but because collectives have very little sense of obligation to others. That is why we have no persuasive grounds for assuming that a society which acts justly at home will also act justly abroad.[51]

What contributes to the disillusionment of the Third World is the failure to come to grips with the reality that the behavior of Western democracies is, at bottom, a reflection of the attitude of their collectivities. Whereas the people of the Third World have learned to expect injustice from their own dictators and from the governments of powerful states, they still seem unprepared to accept that the so-called common folks in the powerful countries may actually support imperialism to preserve their privileges, and that asking global justice from the majority—the middle class—of powerful nations is often an exercise in futility, for it is the middle class that is generally consumed with paying the bills for its own life-style and is otherwise unable and unwilling to look beyond what is presented by television cameras and newspaper headlines. Similarly, the people of the Third World are still unprepared to accept that the middle-class majority in the West has rejected prolonged involvements in foreign wars, not on account of anti-imperialism, but because such involvements were claiming unacceptable casualties, producing no victories, and disrupting the tranquility of middle-class life; that, if faced with serious shortages, it is the middle-class majority that would exert the greatest pressure upon their government to provide additional resources at whatever cost to other countries; and that the imperialism of powerful states is best understood, not as the conspiracy of their elite, but as the consensus of the society below.

The failure to comprehend the political culture of powerful states is most vividly reflected, for example, in the conduct of the Palestinians, the Iranians, and the Irish militants. The staging of spectacular terrorist episodes, such as those at the Munich Olympics and Entebbe by the Palestinian militants, the takeover of the American Embassy and the detention of American diplomats by the Iranian militants, and the assassination of Lord Mountbatten by the Irish militants, represents a desperate attempt to get attention. But more significant, such criminal acts are also a symptom of a profound misreading of political realities. As preposterous as it may appear, the actions of these militants are in part motivated by the belief that the middle-class majority in the powerful nations may overlook the terrorist acts and, against the wishes of their own government, choose to support the militants' cause. Indeed, the conduct of such militants is not merely an act of outrage but an admission of ignorance.

In the final analysis, an understanding of the relationship between the major powers and Third World countries becomes possible only by acknowledging their predicament. This includes recognizing American-Soviet imperial rivalry as the principal force underlying the global political milieu within which all nations must operate. It also includes recognizing peculiarities of individual Third World countries as they relate to their perceptions of world affairs. And, above all, it requires the dispassionate courage to cut through the thick rhetoric of the Cold War and the Third World sermons and to peer across the angry divide separating the major powers from each other and from Third World societies.

2

America's Introduction to the Politics of Iran

America's isolationist impulse, stemming from geographical detachment, a sense of self-sufficiency, and relative security, served to protect the virgin continent from the political and social ills that prevailed in the Old World. Whereas George Washington had sought to school Americans against foreign entanglements, James Monroe decided to warn the Europeans against interfering in American affairs. On December 2, 1823, President Monroe went before Congress and declared separate spheres of influence for America and Europe. In exchange for Europe's abstention from expanding its influence to any portion of the American hemisphere, Monroe promised: "with existing colonies or dependencies of any European power, we have not interfered and shall not interfere." In the same speech, however, President Monroe denounced acts of imperialism and characterized the violation of sovereignty of any independent nation as "an unfriendly disposition toward the United States." Nevertheless, it was understood that the aim of the Monroe Doctrine was to protect the American continent while ignoring the activities of European powers elsewhere.[1]

Despite the official American posture, there were individuals and groups of Americans who journeyed to every corner of the globe and became the unofficial ambassadors from the New World. One such group was the Presbyterian missionaries, and one such place was the Kingdom of Persia.

Prior to the departure of the missionaries, knowledge of Persia was limited to those Americans familiar with the history of the ancient world. The story of the Persian Empire went back to the mists of time, and its general outline was conveyed to the West through the prism of Greek history. The exquisite sensibility of the Greek historians had led to the portrayal of all invading armies as "barbarians." But invasion of other lands by the Greek army was portrayed as the triumph of "civilization." Counter to this view was that of the Persian historians, who did not yield to their Greek counterparts in attempting to distort history. Every Persian victory was glorified beyond all reasonable proportions, and every Persian defeat was ascribed to "bad luck."

Americans, however, generally received only one version of this distorted history—the Greek version. If the Greek accounts of ancient history cast the Persians as villains, the Biblical account was far kinder in that it recorded the efforts of the Persian Emperor Cyrus the Great, who defeated the Babylonians (present-day Iraqis) and liberated the Israelites from their captivity in 539 B.C.

American missionaries were motivated not so much by curiosity about Persia as by their zeal to spread the gospel abroad. They had arrived in Persia by 1830, and the first American missionary school was established in 1835.[2] The Presbyterian missionaries brought doctors and medical supplies to a country that was in desperate need of modern medicine. Although the role of the missionaries was looked upon with skepticism and resentment by the Muslim clergy, the overall impact of the missionaries proved to be a positive one. They managed to convert only a small group, but they created a reservoir of goodwill that eventually led to the establishment of diplomatic relations between Persia and the United States.

As early as 1850 the Persian government attempted to negotiate some form of treaty with the United States. The young Nasir al-Din Shah was consciously looking for a non-European power to balance against the relentless pressure from the Europeans. The American minister in the Turkish capital of Constantinople was contacted by the Iranian representative, and by 1851 the two governments had signed a symbolic treaty of friendship. But the same forces that prompted Iran's desire to seek such a treaty were also instrumental in aborting its implementation. Although the sources of pressure were never clearly identified, the most likely candidates were Great Britain, France, and Russia. In 1854 the Persian government sought another treaty with the United States as a means of protecting Iran against foreign aggression—notably that of Great Britain in the Persian Gulf. But the American commitment to avoid foreign alliances that might entangle the United States in unwanted wars resulted in a rejection of the Persian proposal. The final treaty, signed in Constantinople in December 1856, was the Treaty of Friendship and Commerce, which avoided any military commitment by the United States.[3]

Historians generally have analyzed the attempts of the Persian government to seek American assistance within the context of realpolitik. While the insecurity of the Persian monarchs may be considered the primary reason for their seeking alliances with the United States, the role of America's image as an anticolonial power should not be overlooked. A legacy of distrust left behind by the activities of European powers in Iran, and the benevolent image of America, became the two enduring factors that prompted the Persian leaders to seek American help. Because of the central role of these factors, each shall be addressed separately to provide a general guideline for interpreting American-Iranian relations.

A LEGACY OF DISTRUST

The term *xenophobia*—hatred and fear of foreigners—has been invoked to describe the political cultures of some developing nations. A closer inspection of the meaning of this term reveals the fragility of its application. As the experiences of many emerging nations indicate, the search for legal as well as political and economic independence has placed them at odds with the colonialism of the past and what they perceive to be the imperialism of the present. The grievances of these nations have often manifested themselves in the form of a phobia or dislike that is directed toward the colonialists of the past and the perceived imperialists of the present. Hence, while some of the emerging nations may harbor Anglophobia, Russophobia, Francophobia, anti-

Americanism, or any combination of these, they certainly do not suffer from a case of undifferentiated and indiscriminate xenophobia.

The fear of foreign powers became a part of Third World political culture, not because of some mysterious xenophobia, but because of the experience of dealing with European colonialism. Although the European powers did not invent the practice of colonialism, they certainly went a long way in perfecting the methods of exploiting the mediocre leaderships and the internal divisions of weaker states. In the Middle East, British and Russian imperial policies revived the old fears, created new ones, and left behind a legacy of distrust. In Iran, where the Anglo-Russian rivalry was most intense, the infusion of fear and distrust into the political culture militated against cohesive government by accentuating parochial loyalties.

The origins of the Persian distrust of foreign powers may be linked to internal weaknesses and subsequent foreign interventions. The mosaic character of Persian society and the existence of divisive forces in the nation can be traced back to ancient times. The Arab conquest of Persia in the seventh century A.D. placed the country under the umbrella of Islam, thus introducing further divisions between the conquerors and the conquered, Arab and non-Arab Muslims, and between Muslims and non-Muslims.

In spite of such tormenting divisions, as Arab domination of the Islamic Empire began to wither away, the Persian sense of national identity emerged remarkably intact. A partial resolution of the conflict between Islam and the Persian national identity came about in the sixteenth century when Shah Ismail (1499–1524), the founder of the Safavi dynasty, declared the Shii creed as the official religion of Iran. A century later, absolute monarchy with more or less secular features became the dominant characteristic of the Persian political system. Although the boundaries between religion and politics overlapped in Iran, the influence of the clergy was usually inversely related to individual monarchs' assertiveness and ability to exercise power.

The general tendency of Persian monarchs to equate personal interests with national interests was joined with their perpetual adoption of objectives that were beyond their means. One such objective was the recovery of Persia's former frontiers. Professor R. K. Ramazani has summarized the irredentism of the nineteenth-century Persian monarchs:

Monarchial irredentism was accompanied by a persistent disparity between the means and ends in the Nineteenth Century wars. Fath Ali Shah went into unprepared wars with Russia, Muhammad Shah with the Afghans, and Nasir al-Din Shah with Great Britain. They all insisted on the same goal of recovering Iran's former territories without recognizing the limitations of their power.[4]

The point should be made, however, that, although Persian monarchs failed to recognize their limitations, their willingness to go to war did not always emanate from a sense of adventurism, as the term irredentism may imply. Monarchial hostility toward Russia stemmed from the frightening reality that Russia was consistently swallowing Iranian territories. Faced with repeated Russian invasions, it is likely that even the most prudent statesman would have been compelled to take military action.

As a nation, Iran was compromised from within by a corrupt and oppressive ruling elite and from without by the imperialism of the European powers. The nineteenth-century wars, hopeless poverty, and tired traditions had reduced the effectiveness of the Persian government to a pathetic point. In the words of Lord Curzon:

> In a country so backward in constitutional progress, so destitute of forms and statutes and characters, and so firmly stereotyped in the immemorial traditions of the East, the personal element, as might be expected, is largely in the ascendant; and the government of Persia is little else than the arbitrary exercise of authority by a series of units in a descending scale from the sovereign to the headman of a petty village.[5]

Foreign powers were as much the beneficiaries of Iran's weakness as they were its contributors. Bribery and coercion were the most common methods employed by foreign powers to extract concessions from the Iranian authorities. Various treaties that the European powers signed with Iran during the nineteenth century were indicative of the prevailing state of affairs.

In 1801 Great Britain became the first European power to establish an alliance with Iran. The British initiative was prompted by the desire to protect imperial interests in India, which were initially perceived to be threatened by Afghan irredentism and French imperialism. The treaty between Great Britain and Iran provided for the following points:

1. In case of an Afghan invasion of India, Iran would go to war with Afghanistan.
2. Iran would prohibit France from gaining a foothold in Iran and would seek joint action with Britain against any such move by France.
3. In case of an Afghan or French invasion of Iran, Great Britain would provide Iran with military equipment and technicians.[6]

But when Tsarist expansionism drew Russia and Iran into war in 1804, Great Britain refused to help Iran. By then the threat to India had subsided and the early signs of an Anglo-Russian rapprochement were emerging.[7] Sensing the opportunity, France became the second European power to form an alliance with Iran. Napoleon promised Fath Ali Shah that France would compel Russia to return Georgia to Iran. The major provisions of the treaty signed in 1807 between France and Iran can be summarized as the following:

1. Iran must immediately break all ties with and declare war on Great Britain.
2. If France decided to invade India, Iran would grant right-of-way to the French army.
3. Iran would incite the Afghans to invade India.
4. France agreed to recognize that Georgia "legitimately" belonged to Iran and promised to do everything in its power "to compel Russia to relinquish Georgia."[8]

In 1807, the same year that the Franco-Persian alliance was signed, Napoleon and Alexander met at Tilsit to iron out their differences and form an alliance. Hence, the French promises regarding Georgia were not honored, and the French offer for mediation was rejected by Fath Ali Shah.[9] Soon afterwards, France and Russia were engaged in war. The victory over Napoleon allowed Russia to focus on the conflict with Persia, and in 1813, by the Treaty of Gulistan, Iran was forced to relinquish whatever claim it had to Baku and much of eastern Transcaucasia, Georgia, and Daghestan.[10]

The French refusal to honor the treaty of 1807 with Iran had made the Shah susceptible to British overtures. Once again, the British were back in business in Iran. Between 1807 and 1814 various treaties were signed by Great Britain and Iran. The major provisions of these treaties were as follows:

1. Iran would nullify the alliance with France and prohibit France from using Iranian territory to attack India.
2. If Afghanistan entered into war with Great Britain, Iran would attack Afghanistan.
3. If Afghanistan attacked Iran, or vice versa, Great Britain would remain neutral.
4. Great Britain would assist Iran in case of attack by European powers. Such aid, however, was contingent upon the British judgment that "the war with such European power shall have not been produced by an aggression on the part of Persia."[11]

The opportunity for testing the last provision of this treaty arrived in 1825 when Russia invaded the Iranian territory of Gokchah. The Shah requested British assistance, and this was denied. Great Britain contended that "the occupation by Russian troops of a portion of uninhabited ground, which by right belonged to Persia, even if admitted to have been the proximate cause of hostilities, did not constitute the case of aggression contemplated in the Treaty of Tehran (1814)."[12] By 1828 the war between Russia and Iran had produced the Treaty of Turkumanchai, which permitted Russia to annex the territories of Erivan and Nakhichevan and forced Iran to pay twenty thousand silver rubles as indemnity for "the considerable sacrifices that the war had occasioned to Russia."[13] At this juncture, Great Britain offered to help a bankrupt Iran pay the indemnity to Russia. The British generosity was motivated by the desire to deny Russia further pretext for annexing Iranian territories, and hence to preserve Iran as a buffer between British colonial interests and Russia. In fact, the very reason that countries such as Iran and Afghanistan were allowed to retain a precarious independence, as explained by Richard W. Cottam, was because "Iran and Afghanistan occupied a geographical belt at which the dynamics of Russian expansion and British expansion met. Neither Britain nor Russia could have gained and solidified control there without risking a major war."[14]

The last major conflict of this period, and one that further humiliated Iran, was the war with Great Britain over Herat. This territory had been separated from Persia in the eighteenth century and had become part of Afghanistan. After several unsuccessful attempts, the Persian army captured Herat in 1856. Subsequently, Great Britain declared war on Iran, and British forces occupied the island of Khark and persuaded Iran to sign a peace treaty in Paris in 1857 relinquishing all territorial claims to Herat.[15] This treaty, as was the case with the Treaty of Turkumanchai (1828) with Russia, confirmed Russia's and Great Britain's permanent capitulatory rights, which exempted the subjects of the two nations from Iranian laws and regulations. Consequently, the two European powers secured increasing economic and political control over the internal affairs of Persia.[16]

Anglo-Russian rivalry, which had begun in the second half of the eighteenth century as a result of British imperial interests and Russia's historic march toward warm waters, became an integral part of Persian politics by the end of the nineteenth century. The Persian predicament was best expressed by Lord Curzon, who considered Iran, Afghanistan, Turkestan, and Transcaspia as "the pieces on a chessboard upon which is being played out a game for the domination of the world."[17]

THE IMAGE OF THE UNITED STATES

America's anticolonial posture, coupled with the tendency of American presidents to express foreign policy through a universal set of principles, had sent a message of hope to subjugated peoples around the world. Among the messengers of hope loomed the towering figure of Woodrow Wilson, who once stated: "The world is *run* by its ideals. Only the fool thinks otherwise."[18] In *The New Freedom*, Wilson wrote, "The reason America was set up was that she might be different from all the nations of the world in this: that the strong could not put the weak to the wall...."[19] President Wilson had considered Americans above all other peoples to be "custodians of the spirit of righteousness, of the spirit of equal-handed justice, of the spirit of hope which believes in the perfectibility of the law with the perfectibility of human life itself."[20] Such statements were to become a pervasive feature of American policy pronouncements.

Although the influence of American ideals on the actual conduct of foreign policy cannot be easily measured, their profound effect upon the world should not be overlooked. Ideals are sources of inspiration for youth, especially for the youth of the Third World, who often have but little else.[21] That Woodrow Wilson and John F. Kennedy are perhaps the most respected American presidents abroad is a testimony to the power of American ideals.

The craving for hope on the one hand, and the nobility of expressed American ideals on the other, became the formidable force that carved the savior image of the United States. America was placed upon a pedestal and was judged by a set of standards unprecedented in human history. The failure to comprehend that the intensity of national sentiment imposes narrow limits upon the extent to which a nation can be expected to transcend its own self-interest produced disillusionment in later years.

Reflecting upon the hostage hysteria of 1980, it appears that many Americans were baffled, not so much by the terrorist activities of the Iranian militants, but by the intensity of their bitterness toward the United States. Americans were also baffled by the seeming tolerance of Muslim militants toward the Soviet Union. To understand the behavior of the Muslim militants is to consider that the United States and the Soviet Union have been judged by very different sets of moral standards. The much lower expectation for Russia is due to an existing image of the Soviet Union as a habitual criminal that is always willing to consider and often capable of committing any crime. The traditional image of the United States has been that of a nation committed to the protection of the potential victims of such criminals. Whereas alleged American wrongdoings are perceived as America's betrayal of her better self, Soviet sins are considered normal because the Soviet Union has no better self. Whereas the charges against an acclaimed saint always receive immediate and concerted attention, the misdeeds of a felon are often ignored.

Political activists everywhere have realized that charges of crime made against America draw the largest attention, and they have made conscious efforts to exploit this particular American vulnerability. What Plato referred to in *The Republic* as the "pious fraud" has been used by the critics of the United States to describe American foreign policy. But the inherent irony in all such cases relates to a fundamental truth: It is precisely the purity of the American image that has made it such an attractive target. What makes this target politically irresistible is the expected strong public reaction to alleged American misdeeds.

Politically motivated attacks against the United States, however, have been largely confined to the post–World War II era, which coincided with the expansion of American interests abroad. In the earlier periods, the United States was perceived as a new force on the horizon that could redress global injustice.

The nineteenth-century Persian monarchs were deeply impressed with America's anticolonial posture. The Persians, like other subjugated peoples, wanted to believe that relative freedom from material wants had enabled the inhabitants of the new continent to transcend the bigotry and greed of the Old World. Despite America's distance and disinterestedness, the Persian leaders sought to establish a friendship with the United States to counter the Anglo-Russian exploitation of Iran.

PRE–WORLD WAR II DIPLOMATIC HISTORY

A Republican congressman, Rufus R. Dawes, whose sister and brother-in-law were missionaries in Persia, became a leading force in advocating the establishment of diplomatic relations between the United States and Persia. The first American envoy, Samuel G. W. Benjamin, arrived in Tehran on June 9, 1883, on the sixty-fifth day after sailing from New York. On the ceremonial occasion for presenting his credentials, Benjamin refused to wear the special uniform when at audience with the king. In a report to Washington he wrote: "We have certainly gained in their opinion by having the courage to maintain a principle at variance with an otherwise universal usage. Power in the Old World, and in the East especially, is supposed to demand outward expression to command respect."[22]

One of the first questions the Shah asked Benjamin was whether the United States legation was intended to be permanent or temporary. The American envoy replied, "There was reason to believe the former to be the case." Then, as Benjamin remembered, "[Shah], in the most emphatic manner, desired me to convey to my government his earnest desire that the United States should always maintain a permanent legation in the capital of Persia."[23] The first American legation in Iran consisted of five employees, two of whom were Iranians.

The years 1894–96 witnessed mounting disorder in the Ottoman Empire—disorder that was spreading into Persian territory. The American minister, Alex McDonald, met with the Persian authorities to seek protection for American missionaries. The Iranian government agreed to dispatch a regiment of soldiers to the Azerbaijan province. Later, the gravity of the situation forced American missionaries and other Christians to flee from Turkish territory into Iran. The willingness of the Persian authorities to accept American missionaries and Christian refugees was appreciated by the American government, and Secretary of State Richard Olney sent a note to that effect to Iran.[24]

But the murder of the Reverend B. W. Labaree, an American missionary, in March 1904 led to a brief period of strained relations between the United States and Persia. President Theodore Roosevelt and Secretary of State John Hay demanded the severe punishment of the murderer and all accomplices. In December 1904, the Persian government agreed to pay $30,000 to Labaree's widow immediately and an additional $20,000 if all those responsible were not brought to justice.[25] The inability of the Persian government to apprehend all of the accomplices produced several stiff notes from the State Department. In October 1906, the Persian minister in Washington conveyed the grave concern of his government by pleading with Secretary of State Elihu Root, "to beg that you will be so good as to accede to the peaceful solution of a fine."[26] Root's reply of November 7, 1906, stated: "The United States Government will not accept blood money from the state or from innocent Persians in substitution of its just claim that punishment be visited upon the guilty. It is imperative that they be punished."[27] By 1907 this issue had finally been dropped; the U.S. government had been convinced that the last accomplices had escaped to Turkey and were beyond the jurisdiction of the Persian government.

During the period 1904–6, major political developments were taking shape in Iran. Inspired by the nineteenth-century European constitutional reforms, which had spread to Turkey, a movement began in Persia—spearheaded by the intellectuals, the clergy, and the merchants—demanding constitutional reforms. This movement, which later became known as the Persian Revolution of 1906, was unique in Iranian history because the Persians were accustomed to deposing or assassinating their leaders when their conduct became intolerable. The Persian revolutionaries for the first time did not seek to eliminate their autocratic ruler but merely to curb and control him.[28] Edward Granville Browne has described the spirit of this movement:

> My own conviction is that the mere tyranny of an autocrat would hardly have driven the patient and tractable people of Persia into revolt had tyranny at home been combined with the maintenance of prestige

abroad or only moderately effective guardianship of Persian independence. It was the combination of inefficiency, extravagance and lack of patriotic feeling with tyranny which proved insupportable, and a constitutional form of government was sought not so much for its own sake as for the urgent necessity of creating a more effective and patriotic government than the existing one.[29]

Under pressure, Muzaffar al-Din Shah granted permission for the establishment of an assembly of public representatives (Majlis). The American minister, Richmond Pearson, remained apprehensive about the future of constitutional reform in Persia. He reported to Washington on August 22, 1906:

> The great body of the Shah's subjects have no idea of the meaning of "constitutional government." The Persian language contains no equivalent for "constitution" as we understand the term.... there is no middle class, whose intelligence and interests could form the basis and the guaranty of constitutional government.[30]

In 1907 Muzaffar al-Din Shah died. The new Shah (Muhammad Ali), who was influenced by his Russian tutor, wasted no time in undermining the Persian constitution. This produced the so-called "constitutional crisis" of 1907–9. The American response was total abstention from interference in the internal affairs of Iran. When Secretary of State Elihu Root was notified of the existence of a "state of anarchy" in Persia, he instructed the American minister there: "You can not intervene by advice or otherwise."[31]

America's abstention from intervening in the internal affairs of Iran was not shared by Great Britain and Russia, however. The discovery of oil had added another dimension to the Anglo-Russian rivalry in Iran. The Russian defeat at the hands of the Japanese in 1905 made the Tsarist regime more amenable to reaching a better understanding with Great Britain. In August 1907, the Convention of St. Petersburg led to general agreements between Great Britain and Russia. The decisions affected the fate of Persia. The two powers agreed to divide Iran into three zones: The south was to be a British zone, the north went to Russia, and a neutral zone was to separate the two spheres of influence.

That the United States did not protest this Anglo-Russian agreement was a reflection of the basic tenets of American self-interest and ideals. America had nothing to gain from involving herself in European rivalries.

As for the role of American ideals, it was reasoned, however expediently, that, since the language of the treaty required Great Britain and Russia to "respect the territorial integrity and independence of Persia," America did not have sufficient grounds to protest. The disappointment of the Persian government reflected its failure to comprehend the dichotomy between American ideals and self-interest. The Persian monarch's acceptance of the Agreement of 1907 was related to his fear of the constitutional movement. To save his throne, the Shah was willing to agree to anything. In June 1908, with an Anglo-Russian blessing, the Shah ordered his troops to attack the Majlis (national assembly). This increased the determination of the opposition and resulted in nationwide riots. Muhammad Ali Shah was forced to abdicate, and in July 1909, his twelve-year-old son, Ahmad Mirza, became the Shah of Persia.

Despite strict orders from Washington to avoid any involvement in Iranian affairs, one American, a young Princeton graduate named Howard C. Baskerville, took it upon himself to support the cause of freedom and justice. He resigned from his teaching post in Persia to give full support to the constitutional movement. In the ensuing clashes between the constitutionalists and the Shah's forces, Baskerville was killed; the Persians gave him the funeral service reserved for heroes. Even today his name is cited with respect and admiration in Iran.

America's first involvement in Iranian affairs came in 1911 as a result of the appointment of Morgan Shuster, a Washington, D.C., lawyer, as the Treasurer General of the Persian government. The financial difficulties of the Persian government had necessitated the employment of a financial advisor, and the choice of an American was acceptable to both Great Britain and Russia because they did not trust each other. Shuster's intention of remaining impartial was soon doubted by Russia, however, when, in the face of the unavailability of an American, Shuster hired a British army officer to advise the Iranian army. The Russian government immediately began to disapprove of Shuster and to request his ouster from Iran. The American ambassador in St. Petersburg reported to Secretary of State Philander C. Knox: "Mr. Shuster's selection was particularly disagreeable to Russia, not only on account of his action, but because he is a Jew."[32] In fact, Shuster was not Jewish, and the Russian racist propaganda was intended to incite the racist elements in Iran.

When the Persian government refused to fire Shuster, the Russian ambassador in Tehran delivered the ultimatum to Persian authorities that the failure to dismiss Shuster would result in occupation of Tehran by the Russian army. The Persian Minister for Foreign Affairs sent a cable to Washington explaining that the Russians were "exerting themselves to destroy Mr. Shuster's work and to subject this [Persian] government to such threats and pressure which would destroy the very independence of this country."[33] But America was committed to abstention from the political intrigues of Anglo-Russian rivalry, and the response from Washington was that the "Secretary of State does not find it appropriate to offer any suggestion."[34] Shuster departed Tehran in January 1912, nine months after his arrival. One year later, he published *The Strangling of Persia*, in which he described the depressing predicament of that country.[35]

America's detached attitude toward the fate of Persia was not at variance with the general picture of American foreign policy during this period. The Spanish-American War of 1898 had electrified the American people for only a brief period, without changing their basic isolationist impulse. In explaining the impact of this war, one scholar wrote:

> Thereby the nation unwittingly exerted a major impact upon the world competition for power and inextricably involved its destiny in the courts of politics across the seas and yet remained, on the whole, as attached to its isolation and as contemptuous of the changing imperatives of international power as before the war.... Only an active fear for American security could have turned American minds toward the real political conditions of the international environment. But the circumstances of international relations did not create this fear; instead they increased America's sense of self-sufficiency and reinforced her complacent assurance of physical insulation from the toils of world politics.[36]

Long before the onset of World War I, a small group of Americans led by Alfred Thayer Mahan and Theodore Roosevelt came to the conclusion that isolation was rapidly becoming impossible for the United States. While absorbed in the pursuit of power politics, they reasoned that ever-developing domestic pressures, the acceleration of communications, and several other factors had made it imperative that America assume her share of responsibility in world affairs. As early as 1902, Admiral Mahan (then a captain) had demonstrated his brilliant foresight by outlining the strategic importance of the Persian Gulf in an article titled "The Persian Gulf and International Relations": "The question of the Persian Gulf, and of South Persia in connection with it, though not yet immediately urgent, is clearly visible upon the horizon of the distant future."[37] In emphasizing the security requirements of that region, Mahan stated: "Unhappily, the powers that border the Persian Gulf, Persia itself, Turkey, and some minor Arabian communities, are unable to give either the commercial or the military security that the situation will require."[38]

Mahan's concern for the realities of world politics succeeded in capturing the imagination of only a few, and failed to break down America's cherished isolationism. The general populace and their representatives remained oblivious to the imperatives of international power politics. A remark by Henry Adams in 1906 described the prevailing political mood of America: "The Secretary of State exists only to recognize the existence of a world which Congress would rather ignore."[39]

The outbreak of World War I produced drastic shifts in the balance of the international system by destroying old alliances and creating new ones. Great Britain and Russia had become allies against Germany, and their old rivalry in Iran and elsewhere was subdued for a brief period. However, the October Revolution of 1917 in Russia introduced new tactical approaches into Russian foreign policy. In January 1918, the new Russian leadership denounced all Tsarist claims on Iran and nullified the Anglo-Russian Agreement of 1907. Confronted with the new realities, Great Britain decided to seek another treaty with Persia. This led to the controversial Anglo-Persian Treaty of 1919. The provisions of this treaty stipulated that British advisors were to be in charge of the Iranian treasury and army.[40] The Anglo-Persian Treaty, which was secretly negotiated with a few Persian Anglophiles, was subsequently considered by many Persians to be a document that had made Iran a British colony. This treaty was never ratified by the Iranian Majlis.

America's entry into World War I on April 6, 1917, placed the United States on the side of Great Britain and Russia. President Wilson generally believed that foreign policy among the world powers consisted of communication between civilized men of goodwill and that it was guided by an enlightened public opinion. His conduct before and during the war demonstrated his inveterate reliance upon moral suasion. Far from descending to the use of racist remarks against all German people, Woodrow Wilson had the decency to draw sharp distinctions between the German government and the people of Germany. He repeatedly stated, "We have no quarrel with the German people. We have no feeling towards them but one of sympathy and friendship,"[41] and publicly asked for "peace without victory" to spare Germany from total destruction. President Wilson reasoned that the humiliation of Germany would produce "a bitter memory upon which terms of peace would rest, not permanently, but only as upon quicksand."[42] But the hatreds and passions of the European belligerents, coupled with the political games of Wilson's domestic opponents, destroyed the chance for constructing a new world order.

Wilson's proposal for the League of Nations was particularly appealing to subjugated nations such as Persia, which had hoped, through joining the League, to salvage some degree of dignity and independence. By the end of the war, Persia—whose neutrality was ignored by all belligerents—had sent a delegation to Paris and had requested admission to the peace conference. John L. Caldwell, who was the American minister in Tehran, Secretary of State Robert Lansing, and President Wilson were sympathetic to the request of the Persian government. To the surprise of the American delegation, the British representatives opposed the idea and were able to obstruct Persia's admission to the conference. In the open, the British based their objection upon the fact that Persia had remained officially neutral during the war. But the real reason was their fear that the secretly negotiated Anglo-Persian Treaty of 1919 might be exposed. It was not until the disclosure of this treaty that the American government came to realize the true nature of the British opposition. Secretary Lansing instructed the American minister in Persia to make public the American position:

> You are instructed to deny both to Persian officials, and anyone else interested in this matter, that America has refused to aid Persia. You will also state that the United States has constantly and consistently showed its interest in the welfare of Persia and that the American Mission at Paris several times endeavored earnestly to secure a hearing for the Persian Mission before the Peace Conference. The American Mission was surprised that it did not receive more support in this matter, but the announcement of the new Anglo-Persian treaty probably explains why the American Mission was unable to secure such hearings.[43]

The predominant position of Great Britain in Iran continued until 1921, when the emergence of nationalist leader Riza Khan and the new prime minister, Sayyid Zia-al-Din, put an end to the de facto Anglo-Persian Treaty of 1919.

By 1920, however, the British withdrawal from Transcaucasia and northern Iran had led to the Russian occupation of northern Iran. The Soviet government attempted to sever the province of Gilan from Persia by aiding in the formation of the Soviet Republic of Gilan (1920–21). In protest of the Soviet invasion of northern Persia, the Iranian government took the matter to the League of Nations. Aside from discussing the issue, the League simply revealed its inability to take any action. Confronted with the impotence of the League of Nations, the Iranian government attempted to deal unilaterally with the Soviet regime. Russia's internal difficulties had modified the expansionist ideas of some Communist leaders. Over Stalin's objection, Lenin decided to terminate support for the Republic of Gilan.[44] But the Soviet leadership remained bitter about foreign threats during and after the Revolution, and Russia's vulnerability on its southern border prompted Lenin to seek preventive measures. Hence, in exchange for the withdrawal of the Red Army from northern Iran, Lenin secured the so-called Treaty of Friendship with Iran in 1921. The most significant provisions of this treaty, which even today looms over Soviet-Iranian relations, were as follows:

1. Both nations agreed to prohibit and prevent the military presence of a third party in either Iran or the Soviet Union.
2. If a third party militarily intervened in Iran, or used Iranian territory to threaten Russia, the Soviet government reserved the right to dispatch troops to Iran.
3. Both nations agreed to prohibit and prevent within their respective territories the existence of "any organizations or groups of persons, irrespective of the name by which they are known, whose object is to engage in acts of hostility" against the Soviet Union or Iran.[45]

Even a strict interpretation of this treaty could have provided a pretext for the Soviet Union to invade Iran at will. Since 1921, the existence of this treaty has been a constant reminder to the Iranian government that the displeasure of the Soviet Union could prove very costly to Iran.

By 1923, Riza Khan had become Prime Minister as well as Minister of War. Concomitant with the rise of Riza Khan, the prestige of the absentee Shah, who was in Europe, had fallen to an all-time low. Impressed with the political reforms that were taking place in Turkey,

Riza Khan kept a close watch on the emergence of a republican and secular form of government in the neighboring country. But the abolition of the caliphate in Turkey in March 1924, and the establishment of a secular government, alarmed the Iranian clergy, who began mobilizing against the likelihood of such an event in Iran.

For the first time in Iranian history, a charismatic national leader had emerged who was willing to entertain the idea of a republic and accept the title of president. But the clergy's fear of secular government buried this hope at its very inception. Suddenly, the clergy began closing ranks with the supporters of the Ahmad Shah and mounted a nationwide campaign against the very idea of a republic. Recognizing the influence of the clergy, and the danger that it posed to his political fortune, Prime Minister Riza Khan went to the holy city of Qumm to consult with some of the powerful Ayatullahs. Subsequently, the Ayatullahs of that city sent a telegram to Tehran to inform the public that:

> There have been expressed certain ideas concerning a republican form of government which are not to the satisfaction of the masses and inappropriate to the needs of the country. Thus, when His Excellency, the Prime Minister ... came to Qumm ... we requested the elimination of this rubric [of republicanism]. ... He has accepted this. May God grant that all people appreciate the extent of this act and give full thanks for this concern.[46]

To insure the political support of the clergy, Riza Khan issued the following proclamation:

> It has become clear from experience that the leaders of the government must never oppose or contradict the ideas of the public. ... I and all the people in the army have, from the very beginning, regarded the preservation and protection of the dignity of Islam to be one of the greatest duties and kept before us the idea that Islam always progress and be exalted and that respect for the standing of the religious institution be fully observed and preserved: thus ... it is for this reason that I advise all patriots of this sacred aim to avoid calls for a republic and to unite efforts with me to achieve the supreme objective upon which we are agreed.[47]

The reversal of Riza Khan's position on republicanism began to pay political dividends, and in October 1925 the Qajar dynasty came to an end with the passage of a law to that effect by the Majlis. In December

Riza Shah clocking the Trans-Iranian Railway while his son, the Crown Prince, looks on. December 1938. (Source: Iranian Ministry of Information)

of the same year, Riza Khan was entrusted with the Peacock Throne, and thus was founded the Pahlavi dynasty. The Muslim clergy had imagined that, by virtue of certain constitutional provisions, they could maintain a powerful role in the formulation and execution of laws. The clergy had further assumed that they could prohibit both the possible excesses of the sovereign and the infusion of Western influences, which they felt were threatening Islamic institutions. But they failed miserably to achieve either of these goals. After he ascended the throne, Riza Shah's desire for absolute power undermined the constitution, and his modernization program invited Western technology and tradition to Iran.

During this period, the United States' involvement in Iran was largely confined to dealing with problems that confronted the second American economic mission, which had arrived at Tehran in November 1922. This mission was headed by Dr. A. C. Millspaugh, a Johns Hopkins Ph.D. and an economist for the Department of State. Several factors complicated Dr. Millspaugh's work in Iran. The first was his close association with British subjects, which was resented by the Russian and Iranian authorities. Another factor was dissension among the members of the mission with regard to the division of labor. Finally, Dr. Millspaugh's attempts to curb bureaucratic corruption alienated some of the Iranian authorities and resulted in the refusal to renew his contract when it expired in 1927.[48]

After the departure of Dr. Millspaugh, the Iranian government turned to Germany for help. Thus began the arrival of German advisors and technicians that lasted until the Second World War. Once again, a common enemy induced Great Britain and Russia to become allies and to coordinate their policies toward Iran. They accused the Germans of spying in Iran and demanded the ouster of all German citizens from Iran. The Iranian government dragged its feet in dismissing the Germans and thereby provided the British and the Russians with yet another pretext for invading Iran. On August 23, 1941, both countries ignored Iran's official neutrality and invaded Iran without warning. When Riza Shah was informed that British troops were approaching Tehran, he told his son, "Do you think that I can receive orders from some little English captain?"[49] Riza Shah abdicated and left Iran, never to return.

3

The Emergence of American Interest in Iran

The outbreak of the Second World War set the stage for a gradual but accelerating American involvement in Iran. The process began with the Anglo-Russian invasion of Iran in 1941 and later led to the arrival of American servicemen and the establishment of the Persian Gulf Command in 1943. In addition to the emergence of American-Soviet rivalry, which has been discussed in the opening chapter of this book, factors influencing American-Iranian relations included the condition of Iran during the war and the propaganda war waged against the United States first by the Axis forces and then by the Soviet Union. With the aid of archival data, brief exposés of political conditions in Iran and the role of propaganda are presented at the start of this chapter to provide the proper context for reviewing American policies.

IRAN DURING THE WAR

An entire generation of Persians still had vivid memories of the Anglo-Russian Agreement of 1907, which had carved Iran into spheres of influence (1907–15). The familiar scenario repeated itself in 1941, as the Soviets wielded power in the northern provinces, while the British controlled the south. The war against the Axis forces had necessitated the protection of the oil fields and the supply route vital to the survival of the Soviet Union. Faced with the disruption of their homeland, however, the people of Persia found little consolation in the logic of Allied actions.

The exile of Riza Shah removed the Iranian government's sole cohesive element. Riza Shah's plan to program the populace on the themes of statehood, modernization, and sacrifice for the common good was destroyed by his departure. Those who were led to believe that the country was sound and strong were disillusioned by the sight of foreign troops once again marching on Iranian soil.

The designation of Muhammad Riza Pahlavi as the new Shah merely saved the symbol of sovereignty; in reality it made a mockery of the monarchy. The exodus or execution of independent and capable leaders between 1923 and 1941 had left the country in the hands of a young Shah surrounded by unscrupulous vultures feeding from the skeleton of the Iranian government. Although the young Shah was permitted authority within his residence, power really resided in the British and Soviet embassies, with the Americans playing the role of an improvised and often inconsistent referee.

As a nation, Iran was compromised by the requirements of the global conflict and by its attendant social ills, ranging from the presence of foreign armies to shortages of food and medicine. The arduous enterprise of securing a livelihood was paired with the pain of a conquered people. In the cities and suburbs of Iran—where Russian, British, and American soldiers were part of the landscape—a multitude of Polish and Russian refugees rubbed shoulders with homeless Persians. The Russian fugitives lived in daily fear of being detected by the Red Army, which routinely confiscated their personal belongings in the name of helping Mother Russia's war efforts. As reports by the Office of Strategic Services (OSS) indicate, the Polish refugees in Tehran somehow melted into the population. Some found employment in the city. Many of the girls became barmaids in the American army camps, and some

Mrs. Louis Dreyfus, wife of the U.S. minister to Iran, distributing food and medical supplies in the poorer section of Tehran. 1943. (Source: U.S. Office of War Information)

turned to prostitution. The Persians accepted the Polish refugees as one of the results of war.[1]

Riza Shah's departure from Iran ended a period of strict authoritarian rule. Previously suppressed elements, such as the clergy, began to reassert themselves. Aware of an arbitrary exercise of authority by the new Shah, and sensing an ideological vacuum, the clergy embarked upon a nationwide campaign to enlist Iran's disillusioned souls. Islam was unveiled as an umbrella that would save the destitute and the disillusioned from the showers of shame and subjugation. It was an artful construction—one that camouflaged the clerical drive for elevation in the mantle of nationalism. It was a rerun of the past and a preview of the future.

In the absence of a strong social order, the monumental task of collecting tallage from the peasants had become even more difficult for the landlords because of the preachings of Communist agitators. Concerned with the breakdown of feudal customs, the landowners and tribal chiefs accepted the aid of the clergy. A sensible interpretation of divine law, it was reasoned, could substitute for civil law in subduing the peasants. The preaching of Islam would reinforce the fear of God and compensate for the momentary lapse in man's ability to administer civil law.

The extent to which the overwhelming majority of Persians—the peasants—imposed their sentiments upon national life was quite limited. In the political arena, the majority played a minor role. The certainty of their servitude was to survive all social upheavals. Even the ravages of global war could not temper the tired traditions of Iran's political culture.

The small middle class, fostered by Riza Shah's programs, consisted of merchants, government clerks, teachers, technicians, and some intellectuals. As a group, they had remained so divided that, even after the abdication of Riza Shah, no immediate formation of a cohesive ideology or program of action was deemed possible. While some engaged in underground political activities, many participated without enthusiasm in Iran's economic life. As a class, they were firmly committed to the tradition of silent opposition.

The war period witnessed the reaffirmation of the political predominance of the Iranian upper class. One of the effects of this predominance was their relative accessibility to the representatives of the occupying powers. The Persian aristocracy, in attempting to rescue its elevated station and mindful of the cost of having convictions, often yielded to the temptation of attending tea parties in the British Embassy or having vodka with the Russians. Given the national predicament, it may be suggested that the political theatrics of the ruling elite were exercised on the stage of historical necessity. But in practice, the conduct of men possessed by their own crippling visions of power was often presented as patriotism.

THE PROPAGANDA WAR

When the Second World War broke out, Germany enjoyed an excellent reputation in Iran. She was the only European power without an ugly reputation for imperialism and interference in Iranian affairs. Therefore, the Anglo-Russian pressure on Riza Shah to expel German citizens from Iran, and the use of this issue as a pretext for invading Iran, had contributed to a deep resentment of the Anglo-Russian cause and sympathy for Germany. German propaganda had a receptive audience in Iran.

While the targets of German propaganda varied with the changing conditions of the battlefield, its central themes remained the same. To exploit the gloomy mood in Iran, German messages repeatedly noted that Persians and Germans had common racial roots (i.e., Aryan) and that German victory would be the triumph of all "Aryan people." The works of German scholars were evoked to demonstrate the deep affection of Germans for Persian history and culture. The misdeeds of the British and Russians were dramatized to drive home the message that the Germans would be the saviors of Iran. In the early years of the war, the British were the principal target of German propaganda. "The Germans," it was reported to the State Department in May 1942, "playing on the credulity of the anti-British masses, have been most successful in discrediting the British in Iran."2 In the opinion of Louis Dreyfus, head of the American legation in Tehran, Iranian feelings of comradeship for the Germans and repugnance for the British were "based more on general anti-British sentiment than on any affection for the Germans."3 But there was more to the story. The deference toward the Germans was genuine. Persians were in awe of the technological achievements of Germany. It was the same technologically impoverished culture that later stood in awe of the Americans.

By early 1944, in an attempt to destroy America's favorable reputation in Iran, German radio propaganda was accusing the United States of planning to take over Iran by ousting the British and Russians. It was described as another step in America's drive toward world domination.4 In the meantime, the Japanese were not leaving any stone unturned when broadcasting their propaganda in Iran. The Japanese broadcasts emphasized the spiritual affinities between the Asiatic peoples and told stories of fundamental differences in the oriental and occidental views about life. The spiritual life of the orientals was portrayed as refined, but that of the westerners was depicted as producing only grossness. The broadcasts suggested that the woman's proper place was in the seclusion of the home and that "western life is dominated by sexless women."[5] Americans were portrayed as hypocritically talking about freedom and self-determination while at the same time supporting British and Dutch exploitation of the enslaved East.[6]

The concern over the effectiveness of German and Japanese propaganda became so acute that the British prevailed upon the Iranian government to issue a notice warning the public of the consequences of forgetting that Iran was the ally of Great Britain and the Soviet Union. The British-inspired notice was issued by the Iranian police department and was published by the Iranian newspaper *Ittilaat:*

> The Imperial Police Department notifies the public that inasmuch as the Iranian Government and the Governments of the U.S.S.R. and Great Britain are allied by virtue of the Treaty that has been concluded between them, by reason of this alliance propaganda in favor of Axis Governments and against Allies and/or concealment of nationals of Axis Governments are inconsistent with the interests of the country and in violation of the regulations. The Imperial Police Department will therefore severely prosecute the offenders within the limits of the law and regulations.[7]

British propaganda efforts in Iran centered on giving tea parties in the embassy, showing films, distributing pamphlets, and making radio broadcasts that glorified British victories in the war. While the British succeeded in enlisting the support of certain members of the upper class, they failed miserably in gaining the cooperation of the vast majority. Intelligence reports reaching Washington indicated that, because of the steady accumulation of prejudice against and suspicion of Great Britain, the British tactic "either repels the Persians or convinces them that the British intentions are insincere."[8]

In contrast, Russian propaganda was generally successful, principally due to the strict discipline of the Red Army. Unlike their counterparts in the previous invasion of Iran, during the First World War, these Russian soldiers were generally sober and refrained from molesting the civilian population. Much to the dismay of the American military attaché in Tehran, "The Americans and British have suffered by comparison in the eyes of the Iranians because of their tendency to 'whoop it up' somewhat when off duty." Although neither the Americans nor the British misbehaved according to the standards of their own cultures and the customs of military life, their behavior was offensive to a Muslim population that placed a high premium on abstention from alcoholic beverages. The Iranians generally disapproved of the "sometimes loud horseplay and display of animal spirits of some of the American and British personnel from time to time."[9]

The Russian soldiers were rarely seen off duty, and those who were seen comported themselves "in a quiet, serious, dignified manner."[10] Any digression from such behavior was met with swift and harsh punishment. As an example of the Soviet discipline, it was reported that a drunken Russian officer was found in Tehran by two American military police, who thought to do him a favor by taking him to the Russian encampment. When the military police notified their superior, the American commanding officer, who understood the Russian mentality, was perturbed. On the following morning, he telephoned the Russian headquarters in an attempt to explain the incident. But he was told that it was too late, as the Russian officer had been executed at dawn. Thereafter, American military police were instructed "to bring any drunken Russian officers to the American encampment for sobering up and under no circumstances to return them to the Russian encampment."[11]

The Soviet propaganda machine was in full operation from the very beginning of the war. Aside from the conventional methods of distributing literature, Soviet films, and radio propaganda, the Russians had managed to enlist local Communist agitators to incite the Iranian peasants to oppose the landlords.[12] The most interesting feature of the Russian propaganda was the perpetuation of the idea that Soviet interests in Iran transcended the immediate requirements of the war. There were extensive efforts to show the cultural and "scholastic interest Russia has had, and still does have, in Persia."[13] A pervasive feature of the Soviet messages was the promise that Russia intended to help rebuild Iran after the war.

Ironically, the Soviets were able to use American-supplied food and materials to sustain their propaganda efforts. For example, in December 1943, when food shortages in Iran had produced a public outcry, the Soviets suddenly announced that they would supply Iran with 35,000 tons of wheat. This produced the remark from Iranian officials that "there are some things the Americans and British should learn from the Russians."[14] Of course, what the Iranian authorities failed to acknowledge was that the wheat was originally given to the Soviet

Union by the United States. Later, the delivery of the first installment of wheat was elaborately staged, and the Russians assumed full credit for bringing food prices down. An intelligence report to Washington concluded, "Russia does not hesitate to increase her own prestige vis-a-vis the Persians at the expense of the Americans and the British."[15]

In attempting to win the support of the general populace, Soviet schemes in Iran included methods that appealed to the working class. On May 7, 1944, the local Russian newspaper *Novosti Dnia* printed a "letter from Iranian chauffeurs to Tovarishch Stalin." The letter began with a tribute to Stalin's military genius and went on to praise the achievements of the Red Army. It then proclaimed that "we [chauffeurs] want passionately, and in labor, to help the Soviet people to heal their wounds . . . if necessary we are prepared to give all, even up to spilling blood. . . . " The anonymous author of the letter claimed that the information was gathered from interviews with many chauffeurs.[16] On May 18, 1944, the Soviet chargé d'affaires, on behalf of the Soviet government, presented decorations for "labor distinction" to fifty Iranian chauffeurs for their services in transporting materials to Russia. The *Novosti Dnia* then began featuring the photographs of the decorated chauffeurs in its daily issues. Perplexed by the Russian political theatrics, the American military attaché observed, "This represents another Soviet 'first' for neither the British nor U.S. military has awarded any decorations or medals to the Iranian chauffeurs."[17]

Compared with Soviet propaganda, the American effort in this field was neither extensive nor well conceived. An OSS report, dated December 28, 1943, suggested that the American image in Iran and in the Middle East had suffered because of the poor selection of American films that were being shown in that part of the world. The report indicated, "the lousy part of our films make us out to be moll mauling, gold grabbing, syncopated morons. The Russian pictures in Tehran were way above our average and carefully selected."[18] Another source of ill-feeling toward Americans was created by the high accident rate of Allied army vehicles. Although this rate was not out of line considering the conditions and the Iranians' total lack of traffic sense and rules, it caused resentment toward the Allies, particularly the Americans. But as the American military attaché complained, "The Americans have received more than their fair share of this blame and resentment because the

A U.S. Army truck convoy carrying supplies to the Soviet Union. Northern Iran, March 1943. (Source: U.S. Office of War Information)

Iranians did not distinguish between our trucks and American-made trucks in the hands of the Allies."[19]

The major impediment to the projection of a positive image of America, however, related to the fact that the United States had little voice in the Anglo-Soviet-Persian censorship bureau in Iran. This bureau placed far more restrictions on private sources than on government publications. Hence, the Soviet materials, which were considered government publications, filtered through, while the American publications, being mostly privately owned, were stopped. The Soviets, for example, had decided to ban *Time, Newsweek, Reader's Digest, Life,* and many other American publications. The very little that got through was clipped of so many pages that it was virtually unreadable. Furthermore, the Soviets banned most books on political subjects. For example, Wendell Wilkie's *One World* was permanently banned.[20]

The absence of a strong American initiative to check the belligerence of the Russian propaganda was linked to two factors. First, the ever-consuming Russian concern with the Soviet image in Iran was not adequately understood by the American government in the early stages of the war. Although American policymakers had developed a distaste for Russian propaganda tactics, it was not until the waning years of the war that they began to suspect the Soviets of contemplating either annexing Iran or turning it into a satellite state. But even then, the defeat of the Axis forces remained the primary goal of the United States government. Second, despite Axis propaganda and Soviet schemes, the United States enjoyed a favorable reputation in Iran, which made American officials overlook the propaganda war.

THE ROLE OF THE UNITED STATES

Active American interest in Iran dates from 1942, when the American attitude of distant concern was transformed by the exigencies of the global conflict. In Iran, the United States' lack of predatory intentions and its reputation for philanthropic impulses were well known, primarily because of the dedicated work of the American missionaries. Nevertheless, there were liabilities that militated against the American image. According to American representatives in Iran, the announcement of the Atlantic Charter, which had preceded the Anglo-Russian invasion of Iran by only two weeks, had created the impression that "[President] Roosevelt gave Churchill the go-ahead signal while planning the 'Charter' and that Riza Shah's appeal to Roosevelt for intervention was therefore ignored."[21] Furthermore, the fact that American troops entered Iran without formal agreement strengthened the Iranian "suspicions of our [American] ultimate aims."[22] For Persians, who had feared the Russians and distrusted the British for years, the most disturbing new reality was finding America in alliance with the Soviet Union and Great Britain.

To describe the task of the American representatives in Iran as difficult is indeed an understatement. Amid the prevailing sociopolitical confusion and a relentless propaganda barrage, the American officials had to accommodate the imperatives of the war and deal with their newly acquired allies. The burden of understanding the Russian and British schemes was compounded by the demand of both countries that the United States play the role of an honest broker in their frequent disputes over the control of Iran. Stationed in a war-ravaged country, American diplomats and military officers had to sympathize with the people of Iran. Their sympathy was tested daily by the members of the Iranian government and other groups or individuals who pleaded with the American officials to curtail the activities of the British and the Russians.

The United States' representatives in Iran were always called upon to make judgments and often played the role of confused referee. The often accurate but half-stated reports to Washington at times placed the views of American officials in Iran at odds with those of Washington policymakers, who either misunderstood such reports or dismissed them altogether. The perception gap reflected both the broader geopolitical concerns of Washington officialdom and the relative serenity of the United States during the war. But for American representatives in Iran, their proximity to the ravages of war and their perception of Anglo-Russian misdeeds were all too real to be ignored.

The Tripartite Treaty of January 29, 1942, which was forced on Iran, gave the appearance of legitimacy to the Anglo-Russian occupation. The negotiations for this treaty, which lasted from September 1941 to January 1942, were primarily for establishing British and Russian prerogatives in dividing Iran into spheres of influence. Furthermore, the infamous censorship bureau, which had so effectively undermined the release of American materials and had facilitated Soviet propaganda efforts, was also created by this treaty. The first article of the treaty declared:

> His Majesty The King of Great Britain, Ireland and the British Dominions beyond the Seas, Emperor of India, and the Union of Soviet Socialist Republics (hereinafter referred to as the Allied Powers) jointly and severally undertake to respect the territorial integrity, sovereignty and political independence of Iran.[23]

To reduce the anxiety of Iran, article five of this document promised:

> The forces of the Allied Powers shall be withdrawn from Iranian territory not later than six months after all hostilities between the Allied Powers and Germany and her associates have been suspended by the conclusion of an armistice or armistices, or on the conclusion of peace between them, whichever date is the earlier. The expression "associates" of Germany means all other Powers which have engaged or may in the future engage in hostilities against either of the Allied Powers.[24]

The signing of this treaty did not produce the voluntary cooperation of Persians with the Anglo-Russian forces. If anything, the Persians had learned from many years of experience that signing treaties with Great Britain and Russia had never benefited Iran. The provisions of such treaties throughout the 1800s and early 1900s were invoked only to serve the interests of Russia and Great Britain.[25] Therefore, the Anglo-Russian pledge of non-interference was not taken seriously by the people of Iran. The Persians were not alone in their judgment of the Anglo-Russian designs. The American diplomatic and intelligence reports during the war were studded with negative comments regarding Anglo-Russian conduct in Iran. "Intervention has, nevertheless, continued," said an OSS dispatch. "It would, doubtless, be justified by the Russians and the British on the grounds of military necessity, though an impartial judge might question the adequacy of the reasoning."[26] The purpose of the Anglo-Russian tactics was to influence a large section of the population of Iran "to adopt an attitude of resignation, discouragement, and indifference toward any attempts to revive Persia as an independent and self-respecting nation."[27] Far from being surprised at the reluctance of Persians to cooperate with the Anglo-Russian forces, the head of the American legation in Iran wrote to the State Department:

> This whole affair serves as an excellent lesson in practical international relations. Relations based on force and exploitation rather than mutual help and good will do not pay dividends when the day of reckoning arrives. This is brought more forcefully home by contrasting these strained relations with the cordial ones existing between Iran and the United States.[28]

The British role in sending threatening notes to the Iranian government to speed the expulsion of Japanese diplomats from Iran, and Anglo-Iranian disputes over food supplies and other financial issues, further complicated matters. Iran was already on the verge of breaking diplomatic ties with Japan when the British ambassador in Tehran informed the Iranian prime minister that, if the goodwill of the British Empire was to be preserved, the Japanese legation must be expelled at once and that failure to do so would mean the termination of food supplies to Iran.[29] But as the United States' representatives reported to Washington, the British note was "quite unnecessary for it seemed likely at the time it was delivered that the Iranians would accede to the British-American representations without the necessity of resorting to strong and formal pressure."[30]

British meddling in Iranian affairs was extended to the point of deciding who should be permitted to run the Iranian government. In 1943 the young Shah, in an attempt to deal with the political confusion, asked Muhammad Musaddiq to become prime minister. Musaddiq, who was to become a central figure in Iran during the early 1950s, informed the Shah that he would accept the job only "if the British would agree" and contended that "nothing was ever done in Iran without the agreement of the British." The Shah then sent his court minister to the British embassy to request permission. The British ambassador not only rejected the choice of Musaddiq but threateningly stated that "the King is gambling with the crown."[31] Musaddiq did not become prime minister in 1943. The Shah deeply resented the British interferences in Iranian politics, as indicated in his last autobiography. Recalling the activities of the British, the Shah complained that "the English always talk about the merits of democracy, but found it perfectly normal to dictate how Iranian elections should be held."[32]

Other British schemes, such as arming the Iranian tribes for possible use against the Germans, were deemed dangerous by American military analysts, who warned that such policies would lead to a very serious postwar situation that could result in the disintegration of Iran. In describing British aims in Iran, an OSS report concluded that Great Britain wanted: "(1) assurance that the exploitation of the Iranian oil fields by Britain shall continue after the war, and (2) that outside influences, especially Russian, shall be prevented from interfering in India where the British hope after the war to continue their exploitation. To gain these ends, few sacrifices are too great."[33]

In the eyes of American officials in Iran, the conduct of the other American ally—the Soviet Union—was also unacceptable. Aside from massive anti-American propaganda, the Soviet subversion of American goals at times went beyond the traditional clandestine Russian schemes. In September 1943, a Soviet official in Tehran wondered aloud, "Why should the Persians hire American advisors when we, as their neighbors, better understand their circumstances and needs?"[34] The answer to the question was, of course, self-evident. The Persians did not trust the Russians. Their respect for the United States and the assumed honesty of the American advisors were compelling reasons for the Persians to pay the relatively high salaries of the American advisors.

What emerges from combing through the intelligence and diplomatic documents of the war period, however, is a clear feeling of sympathy on the part of American representatives for the people of Iran. The following was typical of the reports that were being sent to Washington: "The clue to the feelings of anyone except the most casual visitor to Iran must be the sense of pity for the straits into which this past great country has fallen and a desire to aid her revival in every possible way."[35]

In evaluating the American position in Iran, a dispatch dated January 5, 1943, observed: "The favorable position of the U.S.A. remains unaltered and great hopes are still held of moral and material assistance from our country." The report also warned: "But unless some concrete expression of American policy with regard to Iran is forthcoming in the near future we shall be gradually identified with the British."[36] The continuous stream of such reports to Washington, combined with the gradual formation of American global strategies, helped to bridge the perception gap between the United States' representatives in Iran and the American policymakers in Washington, and paved the way for the emergence of America's policy toward Iran.

The actions of the Iranian government were clearly intended to establish close ties with the United States. Iran severed diplomatic relations with Japan in March 1942, and shortly thereafter requested membership in the United Nations. For a country that had been denied a hearing at the Paris Peace Conference because of British objections, this was another chance to join the new world organization. But this time, the United States government informed the Iranian authorities that Iran could not become eligible "merely by severance of relations with Axis powers."[37] In order to become eligible, Iran had to fulfill the requirement of being at war with at least one Axis power. In September 1943, Iran issued a formal declaration of war against Germany and thus became eligible to join the United Nations. The American insistence on a formal declaration of war, which basically questioned Iran's contribution to the war effort, was not well received in Tehran. The Persians felt that Iran had already contributed to the Allied cause more than most of the signatories of the UN Declaration and had suffered more than most of the nations presumably at war with the Axis forces. The Persians were also disappointed by the delay in the United States' assistance, which was granted in March 1942 by the extension of the Lend-Lease Program. It was not until the end of the war that Iran began to receive such assistance. To understand the frustration of the people of Iran, it would suffice to point out that massive amounts of American supplies were being sent to the Soviet Union through Iranian transportation routes. The Persians had to deal with the fact that the resources of their impoverished country were being used to transport supplies to their traditional enemies in Russia at a time when food riots were rampant in Iran. Despite such grievances, the Iranian authorities were inclined to believe that the future security of their nation was contingent upon American goodwill and assistance.

By early 1943, the symbols of the U.S. presence in Iran were already established. In addition to the diplomatic mission, the American presence included the Persian Gulf Command and advisors to the Ministries of Food and the Treasury. The Iranian government also managed to receive permission to hire Colonel Norman Schwarzkopf to reorganize the Iranian rural police. Such permission was granted by an act of the U.S. Congress that allowed armed forces personnel to work in those countries whose defense was of special importance to the United States. Colonel Schwarzkopf, who was head of the New Jersey police force at the time of the famous Lindbergh kidnapping case, was successful in his mission to Iran. In the early part of his mission, the usual political bickering in Iran was avoided, and he did an excellent job of organizing the Iranian gendarmerie.

The efforts of Iranian authorities to invite American involvement in Iran began to receive further attention in Washington during 1943. A State Department document of February 1943 stated, "If events are allowed to run their course unchecked, it seems likely that either Russia or Great Britain, or both, will be led to take action which will seriously abridge, if not destroy, effective Iranian independence."[38] The State Department's assessment, which signaled the closing of the perception gap between the United States' representatives in Iran and the policy-makers in Washington, concluded:

> Since this country [the United States] has a vital interest in fulfilling the principles of the Atlantic Charter and the establishment of foundations for a lasting peace throughout the world, it is to the advantage of the United States to exert itself to see that Iran's integrity and independence are maintained and that she becomes prosperous and stable. Likewise, from a more directly selfish point of view, it is to our interest that no great power be established on the Persian Gulf opposite the important American petroleum development in Saudi Arabia.[39]

In August 1943, Secretary Hull, in referring to the above document, reported to the President that "the political and economic situation in Iran is critical and may dissolve into chaos at any moment." In order to protect American interests, a coordinated action by "all interested agencies" of the U.S. government was deemed essential. In particular, said Hull, it was important to have the support of the War Department authorities in Washington and of the American military commander in Iran to assist the United States diplomatic legation and American advisors in Iran.[40] With the enthusiastic support of President Roosevelt, the first coordinated American policy toward Iran was underway. In October 1943, Secretary Hull, in a meeting with British and Russian foreign ministers in Moscow, proposed a declaration on Iran that was intended to clarify the intentions of the three powers in regard to the withdrawal of Allied forces from Iran. The Soviet Union, however, managed to postpone any decision and insisted that the matter be decided in the forthcoming conference in Tehran.

When President Roosevelt arrived in Iran in November 1943 to become chairman of the Tehran Conference, winning the war was still the paramount issue, and planning for peace remained a future concern. But the idea of a new world order and the role of the United Nations were discussed by Roosevelt, Churchill, and Stalin. The Iranian leaders were hoping, by virtue of hosting the conference, to receive assurances that would safeguard the future of their country. Although this conference provided international recognition for Iran, the Iranian authorities were generally ignored. No one was more indignant than the Shah, who received little attention from Roosevelt and Churchill and who was taken as a fool by Stalin. The last autobiography of the Shah provides an interesting picture of his encounters with the three world leaders. "Although I was technically the host of the conference," recalled the Shah, "the Big Three paid me little notice. We were, after all, what the French called a *quantite negligible* in international affairs and I was a King barely 24 years old."[41] Roosevelt and Churchill ignored the international protocol that required a visit to their host. Instead, the Shah went to their embassy residences. The Shah's conversation with President Roosevelt underscored the triviality of the discussions, which apparently stunned the young monarch:

> Roosevelt stood at the peak of his power that year. Imagine my surprise when I heard this agreeable man asking me to engage him as a forestry

President Roosevelt reviews officers of the Persian Gulf Command at Camp Amirabad, Iran. December 2, 1943. (Source: U.S. Office of War Information)

expert in Iran once his term as U.S. President had expired. What could such a request mean? Did Roosevelt believe the future of Iran had been secured so he could already worry about future problems such as reforestation?[42]

The meeting with Stalin, however, was entirely different, as the Shah remembered:

> While my calls on Churchill and Roosevelt were perfunctory and without real significance, my meeting with Stalin was entirely different. For one thing, he was the only participant who bothered with protocol and called on me, rather than summoning me to the embassy as the other two had done. For another, he was polite, well-mannered, and respectful, not even touching his tea before I had mine. What is more, he spoke about matters important to Iran.[43]

The matters important to Iran were, of course, economic and military aid. With Molotov sitting beside him, Stalin told the Persian monarch, "Have no worry about the next fifty years." The Russian leader immediately offered the Shah a tank regiment and a squadron of planes. The Shah was pleasantly surprised. But a few weeks later, when the Soviet ambassador brought Stalin's terms, it became clear that what the Soviet

President Roosevelt talking with the Shah of Iran at the Soviet Embassy in Tehran. 1943. (Source: U.S. Office of War Information)

leader wanted was for Russian officers to command both the tank regiment and the squadron of planes. Faced with Stalin's draconian terms, the Shah admitted, "It would prove to be my first lesson in Russian duplicity and the hard bargain Moscow drove for every concession."[44] Shortly after the Russian offer was rejected, Stalin's displeasure was demonstrated by Soviet propaganda against the Shah.

Despite such indignities, Iranian authorities were pleased with the declaration of the Tehran Conference, which, among its vague and general statements, proclaimed:

> The Governments of the United States, the U.S.S.R., and the United Kingdom are at one with the Government of Iran in their desire for the maintenance of the independence, sovereignty, and territorial integrity of Iran. They count upon the participation of Iran, together with all other peace-loving nations, in the establishment of international peace, security and prosperity after the war, in accordance with the prin-

Allied leaders at historic Tehran Conference, 1943. Seated, left to right: Joseph Stalin, Premier of the Soviet Union; Franklin D. Roosevelt, President of the United States; and Winston Churchill, Prime Minister of Great Britain. (Source: U.S. Office of War Information)

ciples of the Atlantic Charter, to which all four Governments have subscribed.[45]

The United States for the first time formally and publicly demonstrated interest in the welfare of Iran and compelled the Soviets to sign the Tehran Declaration. General Patrick J. Hurley, President Roosevelt's special envoy to the Middle East, was the principal architect of the declaration. It was a great satisfaction for Hurley—who disliked the British and Soviets equally—to curtail future Anglo-Russian schemes in Iran. Hurley also put forward the proposal to elevate the United States legation in Tehran to the status of an embassy. Although the members of the American delegation to the Tehran Conference felt that the demonstration of American interest in Iran was sufficient to deter the Russians and British from continuing their old habits, Louis Dreyfus, the American minister in Tehran, remained cautious: "I do not wish to attach too much importance to the Declaration. I realize that in many ways it is merely a pious wish and that the proof of the pudding will be in the concrete actions of the powers in the future."[46]

On February 10, 1944, a joint announcement by the United States and Iran declared that the two nations had agreed to elevate the status of their diplomatic missions from legations to embassies. This action was intended to balance the American diplomatic presence in Iran with the already existing Soviet and British embassies. As another sign of American interest, a group representing American oil companies visited Iran to seek possible oil concessions in the northern provinces. The Russians, who considered northern Iran to be their sphere of influence, were alarmed. The Soviets were already fretting about the oil concessions in southern Iran, which were given to the Anglo-Iranian Oil Company (AIOC). Therefore, the idea of having American interests in northern Iran, which bordered the Soviet Union, was simply too unsettling for the Russians. Moscow reacted by dispatching its own delegation to Tehran and demanding oil concessions in northern Iran equal to those granted to the British in the south. The Russians were hoping to achieve their goal by intimidating the Iranian authorities through propaganda. What was the Soviet goal? This question haunted the Iranian government. There was no documented report of oil reserves in northern Iran, and, as the future was to demonstrate, no petroleum was ever found there. The Persian authorities were as concerned with the Soviet fuss over northern oil as they were curious about the American interest in the very same region.

What was unfolding, however, was the opening of the American-Soviet chess game in Iran. As early as 1943, intelligence reports to Washington were indicative of the fear that Russia was not planning to withdraw from Iran. The power of the United States was regarded as the best guarantee against the continuation of the Russian occupation of Iran.[47] By involving American oil companies in northern Iran and thus establishing a legal American interest, both the Iranian and American authorities were attempting to check Soviet designs on Iran. The negative reaction from Moscow seemed to confirm the insincerity of the Soviets' publicly stated motives. As reported by the OSS, "The Russians never expected or wanted any oil concession anyway but planned only to prevent the Americans and British and anyone else from getting any."[48] A report from the American chargé in Moscow, George F. Kennan, also indicated that "the basic motive of recent Soviet action in northern Iran is probably not need for the oil itself."[49]

The head of the Soviet delegation for oil negotiations, Kavtaradze, sought to explain his government's motives. In press interviews, Kavtaradze described "the benefits that would accrue to Iran and the Iranian people if Russia were granted these concessions."[50] The Soviet-controlled newspapers in Tehran advocated granting concessions to Russia, and Soviet agents managed to stage demonstrations in support of their cause. Finally, a beleaguered Iranian prime minister announced that all negotiations for oil concessions were postponed until after the war. By this decision, an early American-Soviet confrontation in Iran was avoided.

The authorities in Tehran informed the public that the United States had expressed respect for the decision of the Iranian government because "Iran is an independent country."[51] But the most important issue was related to the fact that the American oil companies were private concerns and therefore the prestige of the United States government was not involved, at least as far as the Iranians were concerned. The Soviet negotiators were government representatives, however, and the decision to deny them oil concessions was considered an affront to the Soviet Union. In a new series of interviews, Kavtaradze warned that the decision of the Iranian government "was threatening the friendly relations between the two countries" and that "the Soviet Government would have no further contact with Prime Minister Saed."[52] The Russian fireworks had begun. Suddenly, all telegraphic communications with the Russian occupied zone were stopped, as were shipments of grain from northern Iran. Demonstrations were staged in dozens of Iranian cities, and pro-Soviet newspapers blasted the Iranian government. The Russian ambassador, Maximov, refused to sit in the diplomatic box at a soccer game between the Tiflis and an Iranian team, in order to avoid speaking to Prime Minister Saed.[53]

But the Russian temper tantrum ended with the same swiftness with which it had begun. Under new instructions from Moscow, the attitude of Soviet officials in Iran became conciliatory. Yet the Russians never forgave Prime Minister Saed and continued to oppose him. On November 10, 1944, Saed submitted his resignation. Dr. Musaddiq, then a deputy in the Parliament, was designated to become prime minister. Musaddiq demanded the right to resume his role in the Majlis if and when he ceased to be prime minister. When the Iranian Parliament refused to enact legislation to that effect, Musaddiq declined to gamble with his seat in the Majlis, and, as was the case in 1943, his premiership of the Iranian government was delayed. The political confusion in Tehran continued as various political factions searched for another individual to take the thankless job of the premiership of Iran. In the meantime, Iran's socioeconomic problems and the issue of oil concessions were left unresolved.

The year 1945 brought the difficult transition from an inflated war economy to a recession-oriented market. The erosion of the central government's authority coincided with widespread protests in various regions of Iran. The Soviets wasted no time in exploiting Iran's vulnerable position. On January 8, 1945, the American consul in Tabriz transmitted the news of Soviet activities in Azerbaijan and suggested that the Soviet occupation of the Iranian province might be permanent.[54] The Russians contended that their activities were in accordance with the "security" requirements of the region. By Russian logic, turmoil in an Iranian province was directly linked to the security of the Soviet Union. It was the Russian definition of security that compelled Averell Harriman, the United States ambassador to Moscow, to report on January 10, 1945: "The Soviet conception of 'security' does not appear cognizant of the similar needs or rights of other countries and of Russia's obligation to accept the restraints as well as the benefits of an international security system."[55]

Other signs of Soviet plans in Iran were surfacing in the form of pressure on the Iranian government to abandon cooperation with the United States. On February 16, 1945, the Soviet ambassador informed the Iranian government: "In the event that the Iranian Airways Company did arrange to obtain its planes and technical assistance in the United States, the company might as well give up all hopes of being permitted to operate in northern Iran."[56] In March of the same year, Krachevsky, a Soviet military representative, visited Shiraz and openly criticized Iran's military cooperation with the United States. "Stalin had offered supplies and technical aid to Iran but it had not been accepted by the Shah," Krachevsky told the Iranian officers. "If this offer had been accepted an Iranian mission would have gone to Russia where they would have received much more valuable training and much more equipment and supplies than the United States had given them."[57]

Soviet propaganda focused on various ethnic and tribal elements to stir up opposition against the Iranian government. "Russian plans," reported an OSS dispatch of May 1945, "seem to leave Iran in such a state of insecurity that troubles will break out in various parts of the country and be so numerous and scattered that Iranian forces will be unable to cope with them."[58] A memorandum from Loy W. Henderson, head of Near Eastern Affairs in the State Department, warned, "The disturbing developments which are taking place in Iran make it increasingly clear that Iran threatens to become one of the major security problems of the future."[59] Another memorandum, from Henderson to Dean Acheson on September 17, 1945, suggested:

> It is possible that if the Russians gain control of the leadership of the Azerbaidjani [sic] nationalist movement, they may endeavor to ally that movement with other political or racial groups, including Armenians, Kurds and the pro-Soviet Tudeh Party, in an effort to gain the ascendancy over the central Iranian government.[60]

By late September, American diplomats had concluded that the Soviet takeover of Iran "would create potential threat to U.S. oil holdings in Arabia, exclude American airlines from Iran, orient Iranian trade toward Russia to detriment of U.S., and would end possibility of U.S. oil concession in Iran."[61] To deal with the Soviet threat, the United States government attempted to extract a firm commitment from the Soviet Union to withdraw the Red Army from Iranian soil. The American concern had been expressed at Yalta and Potsdam, but each time the Soviet Union had sidestepped the issue with the contention that the matter should be deferred to the end of the war. When Japan was defeated, the Russian excuse was no longer acceptable. In the Foreign Ministers meeting in London in September 1945, the United States forced the issue by setting the deadline of March 2, 1946, for the withdrawal of all foreign troops from Iran. But as time went by, it became obvious that the Soviets had no intention of honoring the deadline. Henderson's prediction of September 17, 1945, became reality in December 1945 when the Soviet Union moved to sever Azerbaijan from Iran by establishing a puppet government in Tabriz.

As the crisis continued, American policymakers arrived at the conclusion that their efforts had failed to make Iran an example of Allied cooperation in the postwar period. Instead, Iran had become a centerpiece in the postwar global crisis and a test of American determination to check Soviet expansionism. The Iranian leaders came to realize that their country was an early battleground in the emerging Cold War. The traditional Anglo-Russian game in Iran was being replaced with American-Soviet rivalry. Unlike the old game, when both Russia and Britain were distrusted, this time the Persians were inclined to believe in the fairness of one of the participants, the United States.

4

Truman against Stalin: A Tale of Three Messages

But when history says that my terms of office saw the beginning of the cold war, it will also say that in those eight years we have set the course that can win it. . . .

The first crisis came in 1945 and 1946, when the Soviet Union refused to honor its agreement to remove its troops from Iran. Members of my Cabinet came to me and asked if we were ready to take the risk that a firm stand involved. I replied that we were. So we took our stand. We made it clear to the Soviet Union that we expected them to honor their agreement and the Soviet troops were withdrawn.[1]

With these words Harry S. Truman, in his farewell address, celebrated the triumph of containment and claimed a personal victory in forcing the Red Army out of Iran. The manner by which Truman influenced Stalin's decision, however, has been the subject of considerable debate. The origins of the controversy date back to statements made by Truman during a press conference on April 24, 1952. The President told reporters that he had to send "an ultimatum to the head of the Soviet Union to get out of Persia" and that the Soviets complied because the United

States was "in a position to meet a situation of that kind." Later on the same day, a White House spokesman explained that "the President was using the term ultimatum in a non-technical layman sense" and that "the President was referring to the United States leadership in the United Nations, particularly in the Security Council and through diplomatic channels, in the spring of 1946, which was the major factor in bringing about Soviet withdrawal from Iran."[2] Despite this clarification, and despite the fact that Truman's remark during the press conference remained as the only public statement in which the term ultimatum was mentioned, it became intimately associated with Truman's stand against Stalin.

Truman's fading memory in later years created more confusion, as he furnished various accounts of what the "message" contained and how it was conveyed to Stalin. In his memoirs Truman recorded that he told Secretary Byrnes to send "a blunt message" to Stalin.[3] An article written by the former president in 1957 stated: "The Soviet Union persisted in its occupation until I personally saw to it that Stalin was informed that I had given orders to our military chiefs to prepare for the movement of our ground, sea and air forces. Stalin then did what I knew he would do. He moved his troops out."[4] Truman reiterated that military action had been a possibility in Iran during a question and answer session with students at Columbia University in 1959.[5] On the basis of interviews with Harriman and Truman, historian Herbert Druks reported that the President communicated directly to Stalin the warning that he would "move the fleet as far as the Persian Gulf."[6] In 1960 Truman told reporters that the message was delivered by Averell Harriman, the outgoing American ambassador in Moscow.[7] Finally, in January 1980, *Time* Magazine printed Senator Henry Jackson's recollection of statements allegedly made by the former president. According to this version, Truman summoned Soviet ambassador Andrei Gromyko to the White House and told him that the United States would use the atomic bomb if the Red Army failed to evacuate Iran immediately.[8]

Such confusion is obviously disquieting to historians who are concerned with the precise details of events. But nevertheless, it should not obscure the substance of the issue—the crucial role of the Truman administration in checking Soviet advances in Iran. Some critics, however, have relied heavily upon this confusion and other contradictory evidence to discredit the late president. For example, James A. Thorpe attempts to prove the nonexistence of an ultimatum by contending that "Truman's persistent refusal either to document or retract his assertion in the face of repeated challenges and contrary evidence discloses a lack of candor and integrity."[9] Although Thorpe's article imparts the general impression that a threatening message never existed, it is also possible to interpret it as merely suggesting that such a message was neither issued nor delivered to Stalin before March 24—the date on which the Soviets announced their intention to evacuate Iran. To interpret it thus is to grant Thorpe's article a degree of prudence that is not clearly stated by the author himself. Thorpe is quite clear, however, in handing out the indictment that "Truman's documents and memoirs are no more trustworthy than those of most presidents and politicians. Indeed, his memoirs may well turn out to be less so."[10]

An article by Barry M. Blechman and Douglas M. Hart reports: "What we do know is that President Truman's version of the 1946 crisis is mistaken in its essential elements. Nothing resembling an ultimatum was issued. No U.S. military threats were made, either verbally or through the movement of military forces. There was not a hint of a nuclear threat."[11] This article is even more ambitious in its claim than the one by Thorpe which appears to argue for the nonexistence of the message prior to the Soviet announcement of March 24. Blechman and Hart contend that "the notes actually delivered to the Soviet Union during the Iranian crisis cannot be called ultimata, nor threats by any stretch of the imagination."[12]

A SURVEY OF HISTORICAL DATA

This survey seeks to delineate the historical context that is essential for a reasonable interpretation of Truman's messages to Stalin—a context that is often ignored by critics who are too eager to indict the late president. Furthermore, by examining various messages sent to Stalin, this survey seeks to establish clearly which specific message has fostered the controversy, for confusion regarding this subject often accompanies the debate and detracts from the substance of the issue.

When Truman became president in April 1945, there was already a great deal of apprehension regarding Soviet designs on occupied territories such as Iran. Allied occupation of Iran began in August 1941 with the joint Anglo-Russian invasion, which gave the British control of oil fields in the south while the Russians ruled the north. American servicemen were later sent to Iran to establish the Persian Gulf Command. Although the Allied forces were bound by treaty to evacuate Iran six months after the conclusion of the Second World War, the Soviets' intentions became suspect because of their continuous efforts to isolate northern Iran from the rest of the country. The Russians had used their presence in Iran to engineer Communist rebellions, which had culminated in the establishment of puppet regimes in the provinces of Azerbaijan and Kurdistan by the end of 1945.[13]

The tame reaction of the United States to Soviet conduct in Iran, as elsewhere, was dictated by the exigencies of war against the Axis powers. As the war began to wane, the disintegration of the Grand Alliance was symbolized by emerging disagreements over the future of occupied territories. In the case of Iran, the American policymakers were inclined to test the Soviet pledge to withdraw the Red Army as stipulated by the provisions of the Tripartite Treaty.[14] The Iranian authorities, however, had no illusions regarding Soviet motives and continually appealed to the United States to designate a firm date for the withdrawal of all foreign troops from Iran. The view of Iranian authorities was supported by American diplomats and military officers reporting the danger of Soviet activities to Washington.[15] The United States' representatives did express their concern at various wartime international conferences, but each time the Soviets argued that the matter of troop withdrawal should be deferred to the end of the war. When Japan was defeated, the Russian excuse was no longer acceptable. At the Foreign Ministers meeting in London in September 1945, the United States and Great Britain forced the issue by setting a deadline of March 2, 1946, for the evacuation of all foreign forces from Iran.

The issue was brought up again during the Foreign Ministers gathering in Moscow in December 1945. When Secretary Byrnes reminded Stalin of the Soviet pledge to remove the Red Army, Stalin countered that the removal of Russian troops from northern Iran would endanger the safety of the Baku oil fields in southern Russia. According to Byrnes, "Stalin gave the weakest excuse I ever heard him make." Byrnes told Stalin that the Iranian government was planning to present the case to the United Nations and that it would be unfortunate if the very first meeting of the United Nations should witness a U.S.-U.S.S.R. confrontation. To this Stalin replied, "we will do nothing to make you blush."[16] Later, whenever the Soviets complained of the United States' support of Iran, Byrnes referred to his conversation with Stalin to remind everyone that the Soviet Union had been warned in advance of the American position.

Although Great Britain's overall role in Iranian affairs was most constructive in assisting the United States to deal with the Soviet threat in Iran, differences in tactical approach produced some disagreements. In January 1946, the Iranian government's first attempt to register a complaint with the United Nations not only displeased the Soviets but also drew objections from the British. Lord Halifax, the British ambassador in Washington, went to the State Department to see Dean Acheson and requested that the United States government join the British in urging the Iranian authorities to abort their plan of submitting a protest to the United Nations. Upon consultation with Secretary Byrnes, Acheson refused to go along with the British request.[17] However, Sir Reader Bullard, the British ambassador in Tehran, single-handedly persuaded Prime Minister Hakimi to accept the British demand to remove Iran's complaint from the UN. In fact, Bullard insisted on having a telegram to that effect drafted in his presence and sent over the British military radio.[18]

The British were pushing the idea of a tripartite commission (Anglo-American-Russian) to deal with issues related to Iran and did not want to risk a public confrontation with the Soviets in the United Nations. But some American officials questioned the British maneuvers. Wallace Murray, the United States ambassador in Tehran, informed the State Department that he believed the British were preparing to make a tacit deal that would give the Russians a free hand in northern Iran and preserve the south for themselves. Murray confided that he was struck by the frantic urgency of British actions and noted: "I . . . cannot help but wonder whether the British have not decided it could be embarrassing to them to have all facts of foreign intervention in Iran aired in UNO. However pure their motives may be, they may realize that to the world public, their dictatorial actions vis-a-vis Iran government and constant intervention in provincial affairs in the south could be made to appear virtually as reprehensible as those of the Soviets."[19]

Whatever the British motives, their plan of creating a tripartite commission failed. The Soviets refused to go along with it, and there was strong political opposition to it in Iran. Dr. Musaddiq, then a deputy in the Majlis, made an impassioned speech criticizing the idea and comparing it to the Anglo-Russian scheme of 1907, which had partitioned Iran into spheres of domination, and to the infamous Anglo-Persian treaty of 1919.[20] Under these circumstances, Prime Minister Hakimi sent new instructions to the Iranian ambassador in London to file a complaint against the Soviets in the UN. The British decision to reverse their position and to support Iran irritated the Russians, who retaliated by calling for British withdrawal from Greece. The Ukrainian delegation filed another protest, against the British presence in Indonesia. The

Lebanese and the Syrians also submitted complaints against the French and British occupation of their countries. Thus, the first meeting of the United Nations turned into a political circus, marked by the bickering of wartime allies over their spheres of domination. In the words of Secretary Byrnes, "the debate that ensued was acrimonious and created a situation conducive to anything but agreement."[21]

A compromise was sought to curb the eruption of antagonism. On June 30, 1946, a Security Council resolution provided that Iran's appeal would remain on the continuing agenda of the council and that both Iran and the Soviet Union were required to report the progress of their direct negotiations. Neither the Persians nor the Russians were particularly pleased with this arrangement. The Persians had learned from bitter experience that negotiations with their big neighbor basically meant accepting the Russians' terms. The Soviets, for their part, were annoyed by the publicity associated with Iran's appeal to the UN and were bitter about Anglo-American interference in what the Soviets considered their sphere of domination. The UN resolution only briefly delayed an early example of postwar American-Soviet confrontation, which had been simmering for some time and was about to be publicly exposed.

The historical context of Truman's stand against Stalin was developed by the emergence of American-Soviet antagonism and its relation to Iran's geopolitical position. By February 1946, the ominous signs of American-Soviet confrontation were becoming public. A series of speeches by Soviet leaders, highlighted by Stalin's February 9th public address, emphasized the Marxian interpretation of history and advocated military preparedness on the grounds that the forces of "Fascism and reaction" were still alive in "bourgeois democracies."[22] In describing the Soviet attitude, George F. Kennan, the American chargé d'affaires in Moscow, reported to Washington: "At bottom of the Kremlin's neurotic view of world affairs is the traditional and instinctive Russian sense of insecurity.... And they have learned to seek security only in patient but deadly struggle for total destruction of rival power, never in compacts and compromises with it." In referring to Soviet tactics, Kennan stated:

> Whenever it is considered timely and promising, efforts will be made to advance official limits of Soviet power. For the moment, these efforts are restricted to certain neighboring points conceived of here as being of immediate strategic necessity, such as Northern Iran, Turkey, possibly Bornholm. However, other points may at any time come into question, if

and as concealed Soviet political power is extended to new areas. Thus a "friendly" Persian Government might be asked to grant Russia a port on Persian Gulf.... [23]

The enthusiasm with which Kennan's eight-thousand-word telegram was received in Washington turned it into a gospel of American foreign policy. Reflecting upon the publicity associated with this report, Kennan himself later acknowledged, "All this only goes to show that more important than the observable nature of external reality, when it comes to the determination of Washington's view of the world, is the subjective state of readiness on the part of Washington officialdom to recognize this or that feature of it."[24] That Truman's administration had chosen to pursue a hard-line policy toward the Soviet Union was given public expression by the Secretary of State on February 28, 1946. As Byrnes later explained in his memoirs, the tone of Stalin's public address of February 9 and the Soviet conduct in Iran were instrumental in bringing about the consensus that there was no longer any reason for minimizing American-Soviet differences. "On February 28," wrote Byrnes, "instead of sending a 'note' I made a speech setting forth our position on existing problems."[25] This method of communication particularly suited Byrnes, who favored enlisting public support through open diplomacy.

The text of Byrnes's speech, which was delivered before the Overseas Press Club in New York, had been reviewed in advance by and had received high praise from Truman. The central theme of this address emphasized the United States' determination to defend the UN Charter as the most important contribution to world peace.[26] According to Byrnes, the following portion of the speech was specifically tailored to remind Stalin of their conversation in Moscow concerning the danger of maintaining Soviet troops in Iran:

> We have no right to hold our troops in the territory of other sovereign states without their consent and approval freely given.... We must not conduct a war of nerves to achieve strategic ends. We do not want to stumble and stagger into situations where no power intends war but no power will be able to avert war.... If we fail to work together there can be no peace, no comfort and little hope for any of us.[27]

Apparently, this public warning was not heeded by Stalin, who chose to ignore the March 2nd deadline for removing Soviet troops from Iran. On the evening of March 2, the Iranian ambassador in Washington urgently requested United States assistance. On March 4, Truman met with Byrnes to discuss the consequences of Soviet conduct. At this meeting, Truman decided that the "Russian government ought to be informed on how we felt about this kind of conduct in international relations." Truman instructed Byrnes to prepare a message to be sent to Moscow.[28]

On the following day, March 5, 1946, the President accompanied the former British prime minister, Winston Churchill, and introduced him to the audience in Fulton, Missouri. Churchill's Fulton Address, which added the phrase "Iron Curtain" to the rapidly expanding rhetoric of the Cold War, depicted the Soviet Union as the evil force threatening world peace. Truman's presence gave the impression that the United States government approved of Churchill's statements. The fact that several administration officials, including Truman, had advance knowledge of the content of Churchill's presentation vindicated *Time*'s description of the speech as a "magnificent trial balloon" designed to test the reaction of the American public.[29]

Most observers regarded Churchill's anti-Soviet statements as a public expression of what the administration thought privately. But for an administration that had preached the importance of international cooperation, Churchill's call for a "fraternal association of English-speaking peoples" proved to be embarrassing and elicited negative reactions. A joint statement by Senators Claude Pepper, Harley M. Kilgore, and Glen Taylor criticized Churchill's inability to free his mind "from the roll of the drums and flutter of the flag of empire." Churchill's ideas, they warned, would "cut the throat" of the United Nations. Mrs. Franklin D. Roosevelt publicly chided Churchill for implying that English-speaking peoples could get along without the rest of the world, and demonstrators in New York chanted, "Don't be a ninny for imperialist Winnie!"[30]

Churchill appeared disturbed by the picketing outside his New York hotel when General Walter Bedell Smith paid him a visit. "Mark my words," Churchill declared, "in a year or two years, many of the very people who are now denouncing me will say, 'How right Churchill was.'"[31] In fact, Churchill's timetable proved somewhat conservative, for the change in American attitude was emerging faster than he predicted. The manner in which the Truman administration chose to deal with the Iranian crisis of 1946 left no doubt regarding the administration's willingness to confront the Soviets and thus make Iran an early test of containment.

President Truman and former British prime minister Winston Churchill en route to Fulton, Missouri, where Churchill was to deliver his historic address. March 1946. (Source: New York Times Photos)

On the same day Churchill spoke at Fulton, Secretary Byrnes dispatched a note to Moscow, which was delivered to Soviet authorities by George F. Kennan on March 6. In Washington, the State Department immediately released the text of the message to the press, without waiting for the Soviet reply.[32] This message said in part that "the decision of the Soviet government to retain Soviet troops in Iran beyond the period stipulated by the Tripartite Treaty has created a situation with regard to which the government of the United States, as a member of the United Nations and as a party to the declaration regarding Iran dated December 1, 1943, can not remain indifferent."[33] There was no official Soviet reply; instead, the Russians began hammering away at Churchill for the Fulton speech and criticized Truman for sponsoring it. In Truman's words, "The Russians had resorted to the old game of kicking up the dust when you do not want the other fellow to see too well."[34]

Truman, however, prided himself on being able to see that, "if the Russians were to control Iran's oil, either directly or indirectly, the raw material balance of the world would undergo a serious loss for the economy of the western world." The concern in Washington was intensified by intelligence reports indicating that the Soviets had imposed roadblocks to isolate Azerbaijan from Iran and that the Red Army was moving toward Tehran. On the basis of these developments, and the absence of a Soviet reply to the message of March 6, Truman made his move, as recorded in his memoirs: "Then I told Byrnes to send a blunt message to Premier Stalin. On March 24 Moscow announced that all the Russian troops would be withdrawn from Iran at once."[35]

The second message was sent to Moscow on March 8. The day before, a large map of Azerbaijan was taken to Secretary Byrnes's office to show Soviet troop movements. According to Edwin M. Wright, who presented the map, Secretary Byrnes commented that it seemed clear that the Soviets were adding military invasion to political subversion in Iran; and, beating one fist into the other hand, Byrnes adjourned the meeting by stating, "Now we'll give it to them with both barrels." Evaluation of Soviet activities continued on the morning of March 8 in a meeting in which Dean Acheson, Alger Hiss, Ben Cohen, Charles Bohlen, and Loy Henderson were present. All agreed that the Soviets were determined to present Iran and the rest of the world with a *fait accompli.* What was to be the United States' response? Dean Acheson, then the Undersecretary of State, proposed that the United States let the Soviet Union know emphatically that it was aware of the Soviet moves, but that it "leave a graceful way out" if it desired to avoid a showdown. Later the same day, George Kennan was instructed to inform the Soviet authorities that "the government of the United States desires to learn whether the Soviet government, instead of withdrawing Soviet troops from Iran as urged in the embassy's note of March 6, is bringing additional forces into Iran. In case Soviet forces in Iran are being increased, this government would welcome information at once regarding the purposes therefor."[36]

In conjunction with this note, a symbolic message was conveyed in the form of an announcement by the Navy Department that the battleship USS *Missouri* would sail to Istanbul to return home the remains of the Turkish ambassador, who had died in Washington.[37] Although the note of March 8 was stronger than the one delivered on March 6, it still had the characteristics of an inquiry rather than a threat. Furthermore, this message was sent to the People's Commissar for Foreign Affairs, whereas Truman had specifically identified Stalin as the recipient of his message. In short, it appears that at this juncture a message that could be interpreted as a threat had not yet been issued.

To increase the pressure on the Soviets, the State Department began releasing to the press the news of Soviet military activities. On March 13, the *New York Times* reported that heavy Russian columns were moving into Iran. The next day, the headline read, "Soviet Tanks approach Teheran."[38] To counter the unwanted publicity, the official Soviet news agency, TASS, immediately and categorically denied the validity of these reports.[39] By continuing to focus on Churchill's speech, the Soviet propaganda apparatus was seeking to prepare the Soviet public for accepting the notion that the controversy over Iran was part of the Anglo-American conspiracy against the U.S.S.R. "In light of such interpretation," George Kennan informed the State Department, "subsequent Soviet actions in Iran can be portrayed, when time comes, as general measure of security on the part of a Russia hemmed in by threatening aggressors."[40]

Throughout this period, bilateral negotiations between the Soviet and Iranian governments had produced no concrete results. The inability of his government to deal with the crisis had resulted in Hakimi's resignation, thus paving the way for Ahmad Qavam, an experienced politician, to become prime minister of Iran. Qavam emerges from the historical record as something of an enigma. Everyone seemed to find some reason to distrust him. The Shah constantly fretted that Qavam might hand the country over to the Communists. The Russians came to think of Qavam as a double-crosser and an Anglo-American stooge. The American diplomats thought he was a shrewd politician and often questioned his motives, and the British referred to him as that "sly old bird." The fact that everyone suspected him was perhaps a testimony to his keen intelligence and essential patriotism. But in pursuing his goals, very much like political figures elsewhere, Qavam was capable of playing a cunning game whenever it served the interests of his country. During talks in Moscow, both Stalin and Molotov complained that Iran had discriminated against the Soviet Union by granting oil concessions to the British but refusing them to the Russians. To avoid provoking the Soviet leaders, Qavam explained that he was prohibited by law from discussing the question and that the only hope of reopening the issue lay in the election of a new Majlis, which was impossible as long as foreign troops (the Red Army) remained in Iran. When Molotov pressed for Iran's recognition of an independent Azerbaijan, Qavam did not argue but once again politely explained that such recognition required approval from a new parliament, the formation of which was delayed by the presence of Soviet troops. As subsequent events were to testify, Qavam had no intention of satisfying Soviet wishes and was merely seeking to induce the departure of Soviet troops.

In addition to threatening Qavam with grave consequences if Soviet demands were not met, Stalin took it upon himself to lecture Qavam about the importance of introducing social reforms in Iran. The idea appealed to Stalin because such reforms would have uprooted Iran's feudal system, thus allowing the establishment of a new labor force susceptible to Communist manipulation. To stress the necessity of reform, Stalin told Qavam that England would not have lost America had she made reforms there, and that she would lose India if she once again neglected the need for reforms. Qavam tactfully agreed that social reforms were indeed important but added, "This would be possible only if Iran were left alone." Later, in describing the experience of dealing with Stalin, Qavam confided, "when dealing with a lion you must cajole it and feed it, not attempt to match your claws against his."[41]

In contrast to Secretary Byrnes, who could rely upon the power of the United States to embarrass the Soviets publicly, Qavam shied away from provoking Iran's big neighbor. In the judgment of the American ambassador, "Qavam was an old school politician who wanted somebody else to test out how many army divisions world opinion was worth." It took a concerted effort on the part of American diplomats to make Qavam realize that publicizing Iran's case in the United Nations was the best course of action. To understand Qavam's position, it suffices to point out that just the rumors of Iran's new initiative to complain to the UN were enough to bring the Soviet warning that "this would be regarded as an unfriendly and hostile act and would have unfortunate results for Iran." But a few hours later came the American advice that "there is nothing in the circumstances for Iran to do but immediately to file an appeal with the Security Council." This occurred on March 15. The tightrope-walking Qavam was then told on March 17 that the British attitude was identical to that of the United States. Qavam's decision was publicly announced on March 19, when Iran's representative to the UN requested that the dispute be placed on the agenda of the Security Council, which was to meet on March 25 in New York.[42]

The Soviets promptly proposed to change the date of the Security Council meeting from March 25 to April 10. The British thought the Russian game was to delay the hearing of the dispute until the matter could be "fixed." Secretary Byrnes arrived at a similar conclusion, and in addition to rejecting the Soviet proposal, he initiated an American resolution that placed the consideration of Iran's case at the head of the Security Council agenda. To erase any lingering doubts, President Truman, at a press conference on March 21, attested to America's determination to seek an immediate review of Iran's complaint by the United Nations. On March 24, a day before the Security Council was to meet, the Soviets announced their willingness to withdraw troops from Iran within five to six weeks "if nothing unforeseen should take place."[43]

Although the Soviet announcement could hardly be considered as the end of the crisis, it was indeed the first sign of a softening Soviet position. The Truman administration interpreted this development as the positive result of "getting tough" with the Soviets. Secretary Byrnes also perceived it as a vindication of the significance of public opinion and claimed, "The Soviets could not stand the spotlight." To keep the focus on the Soviets, Byrnes rejected a new Soviet attempt to remove Iran's complaint from the UN by arguing that the terms of the Russian promise were not clear enough and that the Iranian government had not confirmed any accord. On March 27, after the council had voted to leave the matter on the agenda, Andrei Gromyko, Russia's representative at the UN, dramatically walked out of the chamber, the first time a member of the Security Council had indulged in such an exercise. One week later, however, another positive sign came, in the form of the Soviet-Iranian agreement of April 4, which called for the removal of Soviet troops by early May. Once again the Soviets argued that in light of the new agreement Iran's case should be dropped. But again Byrnes refused, insisting that there should be no strings attached to the withdrawal of the Russian forces. Finally, on April 14, the Soviets conceded that "evacuation would be completed unconditionally by May 6."[44]

There is no doubt that the Soviet announcement of March 24, the Russian-Persian agreement of April 4, and the Soviet agreement of April 14 to withdraw troops unconditionally were all induced by the continuous pressure of the Truman administration. The remaining question, however, is whether or not a threatening message followed the notes of March 6 and March 8 and subsequently influenced Stalin's decisions. Seeming to deny the existence of such a message is a body of evidence that is often partially noted by various authors and that is heavily emphasized by those seeking to discredit Truman.

The most commonly cited evidence is an editorial note appearing in one of the volumes of *Foreign Relations of the United States* that indicates that "no documentation on the sending of an ultimatum to the Soviet Union has been found in the [State] Department files, or in the files of the Department of Defense, nor have several of the highest officers of the Department in 1946 been able to affirm the sending of an ultimatum."[45] Both Averell Harriman and George Kennan later denied having any knowledge of a threatening message to Stalin. When questioned by reporters in 1960, Harriman explained that he had left Moscow in March 1946 and was traveling through the Far East, and George Kennan stated, "I was Charge d'Affaires until April or May of 1946. I don't recall anything about the note. I don't know how he [Truman] could have sent it. Perhaps it was after my time."[46]

In addition to the fact that neither Secretary Byrnes nor Dean Acheson has mentioned the message in their memoirs, there is a letter from George Allen, assistant director of the Office of Near Eastern Affairs in March 1946, that places Secretary Byrnes and Allen Dulles among the American officials who could not remember such a message.[47] There is also a reported account that Loy Henderson, chief of the Office of Eastern European Affairs in 1946, confided that as far as he knew "Truman never sent an admonitory message to Stalin."[48]

AN ASSESSMENT

As stated earlier, the critics have relied upon the contrary evidence and the confusion stemming from Truman's fading memory to discredit the claim that a threatening message was sent to Stalin. Whereas Thorpe sought to prove the nonexistence of such a message prior to the Soviet announcement of March 24, Blechman and Hart contend that it never existed. To challenge the assertions of both articles, the issue may be addressed in the form of the following questions: (1) Was there a third message before March 24? (2) Was it strong enough to constitute a threat? (3) Was it conveyed to Stalin prior to March 24? (4) Did the message influence the outcome of the crisis?

On the basis of evidence that shall be presently detailed, it is the judgment of this writer that the answers to the first, second, and fourth questions are affirmative. But by the time the message was delivered to Stalin, the continuous pressure of the Truman administration, as described in the preceding pages, had extracted the initial Soviet announcement of March 24. What is being suggested here is that Truman had issued the message *before* the initial Soviet declaration and that *after* it was conveyed to Stalin it played a crucial role in bringing about the Soviet-Iranian agreement of April 4 and the subsequent Soviet concession to withdraw troops unconditionally.

To begin with, there is evidence that indicates the President gave a message to General Walter Bedell Smith, the new American ambassador to Moscow, on March 23, the day *before* the initial Soviet announcement. This fact is revealed by a note Truman left on his appointment calendar, next to the entry of Smith's appointment, which states: "I told him to tell Stalin I had always held him to be a man to keep his word. Troops in Iran after March 2 upset that theory." Although the note on the calendar does not fully expose the serious nature of Truman's message, it does indicate that the President also told Smith to offer a conciliatory gesture by inviting the Soviet leader to visit the United States. Furthermore, since the calendar also shows that Truman's meeting with Smith was "off the record," this may explain why other State Department officials were not aware of this message.[49]

The proposition that Truman might have later fabricated evidence to support his claim has been suggested by James Thorpe. However, the memoirs of Ambassador Smith—which curiously enough have not been mentioned in any of the articles referred to in this study—refute Thorpe's allegations. In *My Three Years in Moscow,* Smith recorded the following information: (1) He had two conversations with Truman before he left for Moscow, during which the President gave him a message to deliver to Stalin and instructed him "to ask some very direct questions"; (2) that Truman wanted to confront Stalin using the carrot-stick approach is indicated by Smith's reference to the fact that the President also instructed him to invite Stalin to visit the United States; (3) Smith left Washington on the morning of March 24, thus lending credence to Truman's diary entry, which recorded a meeting with Smith on March 23.[50]

Upon his arrival in Moscow, Smith informed the Soviet authorities that he had a message from Truman and secured an interview with Stalin for the evening of April 4. Smith's description of the hour before he met Stalin speaks volumes:

> I had believed myself more or less immune to excitement, after the stress and strains of more than four years of war, but I must confess that I experienced a mounting feeling of tension as the hour for the interview with Stalin approached. I thought the meeting might be a stormy one, and for that reason I chose to go alone, not taking any of my senior Embassy officers or even an interpreter with me. Mr. George Kennan, then our Minister-Counselor in Moscow, who had been in the Soviet Union for extended periods since our first diplomatic mission was established in 1933, and other Embassy officers, dined with me at Spaso House that night, but we did more talking than eating as we tried to anticipate the course of the coming conversation, the importance of which we felt strongly.[51]

Smith's dramatic description, apart from revealing the serious nature of his mission, also calls into question the validity of statements made by George Kennan. It is rather odd that after the experience of that evening Mr. Kennan could not remember anything about the message. In particular, Kennan's statement that "I don't know how he [Truman] could have sent it" becomes highly questionable. Furthermore, the fact that Smith's meeting with Stalin was after the Soviets had made the initial announcement of March 24 gives special significance to Smith's anxiety. If anything, one would expect that the Soviet announcement would have allowed Smith to soften the tone if not the substance of the message he gave to Stalin. In Smith's words:

> The President had asked me to say that both he and Secretary Byrnes had always believed that when the Generalissimo made a statement or a commitment he meant to keep it, and the American people hoped that events would confirm that belief, but it would be misinterpreting the character of the United States to assume that because we are basically peaceful and deeply interested in world security, we are either divided, weak or unwilling to face our responsibilities. If the people of the United States were ever to become convinced that we are faced with a wave of progressive aggression on the part of any powerful nation or group of nations, we would react exactly as we have in the past.[52]

The determination of whether the above message constitutes a threat, however subjective it may be, is still related to the objective realities of 1946. After all, what makes any threat persuasive is the perception of the power required to carry out the threat and the willingness to use that power. In 1946, despite the demobilization process, the United

States was perceived to be the greatest military power in the world. As for the willingness to use that power, it may be suggested that any sane government must have taken seriously the slightest hint of a threat by a man who some months earlier had ordered atomic bombs dropped on Hiroshima and Nagasaki. In addition, as disclosed by a public-opinion poll taken in mid-March of 1946, Truman had the overwhelming support of the American public to confront the Soviets.[53] Therefore, considering the historical context, Truman's message—that if faced with progressive aggression "we would react exactly as we have in the past"—had indeed all the makings of a very strong threat.

Before documenting the role of this message, some final comments regarding the critics who have denied its very existence are in order. In light of the foregoing presentation, it is reasonably clear that the conclusions put forward by Thorpe and by Blechman and Hart are not supported by the available evidence. The curious fact, however, is not so much that the critics interpreted Truman's message as non-threatening, but rather that they failed to present the message itself, which is contained in *Foreign Relations of the United States, 1946* (vol. 6, p. 733). For example, Thorpe—who accuses Truman of a lack of candor and integrity—not only fails to disclose anything about the message that Ambassador Smith conveyed to Stalin, but he also omits any mention of Truman's appointment calendar and the account of Smith's memoirs.

The article containing the most serious flaws, however, belongs to Blechman and Hart, who argue, "The notes actually delivered to the Soviet Union during the Iranian crisis cannot be called ultimata, nor threats by any stretch of the imagination." This statement may reveal something about the perceptions of the authors, but, again, it does not explain why they fail to present the text of the message actually delivered to Stalin by Ambassador Smith. To say the least, such an omission makes it difficult for readers to decide for themselves whether or not Truman's message contained a threat.

That Blechman and Hart also fail to mention Smith's memoirs is even more curious than the similar omission by Thorpe because they do refer to Truman's appointment calendar and thus are aware of the President's meeting with Smith. Instead, Blechman and Hart refer to the appointment calendar only to produce an interpretation that defies logic. It is hard to believe, they contend, that Truman would combine a threatening message with a conciliatory gesture.[54]

First, why is it hard to believe that Truman would employ such a method? After all, the carrot-stick approach is a time-tested and viable political tool. Second, had the authors consulted Smith's memoirs, they might have noticed that Smith's anxiety was not that of a man who merely wanted to extend an invitation to Stalin. Finally, nowhere in the Blechman and Hart article is the inadequacy of their research more vividly demonstrated than in the following statement:

> On 21 May Iranian troops entered Azerbaijan and reported the complete removal of Soviet men and equipment. Having verified Soviet compliance with the April agreement, the Iranians promptly broke it. Their army marched on Tabriz and removed the Soviet-installed government; a short time later, the Iranian legislature repudiated the joint stock arrangement.[55]

It suffices to point out that the Iranian army did not march on Tabriz in May of 1946. In fact, it was not until seven months later, in December of 1946, that such an event took place. As shall be described later, the seven months between the Soviets' withdrawal and the return of Azerbaijan to Iran constituted a most trying period for the Iranian authorities, who finally decided to dispatch troops after repeated assurances of support were given by the Truman administration.

FROM TRUMAN'S MESSAGE TO THE END OF THE CRISIS

To appreciate the role of Truman's message, we must consider Soviet conduct prior to Smith's arrival in Moscow. Despite continuous American and British efforts in the United Nations, and the notes of March 6 and March 8, there was no significant change in the Soviet attitude. Although the Soviet announcement of March 24 did signal a softening in position, at bottom it was merely an effort to deal with the pressure of world opinion expressed in the United Nations. As an archival record reveals, "on March 25, Soviet troops, instead of evacuating, moved to within 23 miles of Tehran and literally leveled guns at the capital until promise of an oil concession was obtained."[56] Furthermore, the so-called bilateral negotiations in Moscow and Tehran had been marred by repeated Soviet threats against Iran and had not produced any concrete results.

Such were the circumstances when Ambassador Smith arrived in Moscow and informed the Soviet authorities that he had an urgent message from President Truman for Stalin. Anticipating the purpose of Smith's mission, the Soviets instructed their ambassador in Tehran to proceed with the negotiations but to wait for final word from Moscow. Smith had a long interview with Stalin on the evening of April 4. In addition to delivering Truman's direct message, Smith told Stalin that the most important question in the minds of the American people was "What does the Soviet Union want and how far is Russia going to go?" The American people, Smith continued, understood Russia's desire for security but deplored Soviet methods of attaining it, and recent events in the Near East and in the sessions of the UN Security Council had created grave apprehension in the United States regarding Soviet motives.

Stalin listened patiently, as he took an occasional puff from a long Russian cigarette and drew with a red pencil what appeared to be lopsided hearts with a small question mark in the middle. Then he began to reply in detail. The length and the sequence of his reply made Smith wonder whether Stalin was blessed with a remarkable memory and great power of concentration, or whether the Soviets had already anticipated all the issues that would be raised by the United States. Stalin's statement included a number of countercharges against the United States, bitter complaints against Churchill's Fulton speech, allegations of Anglo-American conspiracies against Russia, and resentment over American support of Iran. Stalin went on to discuss the long history of Persian-Russian relations and complained about the obstacles to obtaining oil concessions.

Smith asserted that the United States had no desire to deny Russia the right to compete for oil concessions in Iran, but that the Soviet methods for obtaining such concessions were unacceptable. Reverting to his initial line of questioning, Smith asked again, "How far is Russia going to go?"

Looking directly at the American ambassador, Stalin replied, "We are not going much further." Aware of the fact that Iran's Azerbaijan bordered Turkey, Smith decided to pursue the subject. "You say not much further," Smith observed, "but does that 'much' have any reference to Turkey?" Stalin carefully replied that, although Russia had no aggressive plan, the Turkish government was "unfriendly" and too weak to protect the straits. That was the reason, Stalin suggested, that the Soviet Union had demanded a base in the Dardanelles to safeguard Russia's security. The Soviet leader seemed to agree with Smith's suggestion, however, that it was possible for the United Nations to provide such security and to avert conflict. Toward the conclusion of the meeting, Smith summarized his remarks and repeated the substance of Truman's message. The meeting ended with Stalin declining an invitation to visit the United States and citing poor health as the reason.[57]

In Tehran, Soviet ambassador Sadchikov and Prime Minister Qavam spent the entire night of April 4 waiting for final word from Moscow. Finally, the tired diplomats signed an agreement at 4:00 A.M. on April 5 (though the document itself was dated April 4). This accord called for Soviet withdrawal from Iran by early May and the formation of a joint Persian-Russian company for oil exploration. The document also stated that Azerbaijan was purely an internal problem of Iran's that would be settled directly by the Iranian government with the inhabitants of that province.[58]

There is additional evidence that indicates the Soviets did not make their final decision until Smith's interview with Stalin was concluded. At a dinner party given by Secretary Byrnes in late April of 1946, both Molotov and Vishinsky admitted during the course of conversation that the Soviets had not decided on the Iranian issue until April 5, thus indirectly confirming the influence of what Smith told Stalin on the evening of April 4.[59]

Both the American and the Iranian authorities continued to monitor Soviet activities. Secretary Byrnes kept the issue alive in the UN by arguing that "withdrawal of troops from Iran without condition was the only sane method to follow."[60] Qavam, on the other hand, was deliberately evasive in order to avoid offending either the Americans or the Russians. When, on April 14, the Soviets conceded through their ambassador in Tehran that the evacuation of the Red Army was "unconditional," Qavam felt that he had no choice but to reverse an earlier decision and to withdraw Iran's complaint from the UN. Secretary Byrnes still insisted that the issue must remain on the UN agenda until the last Russian soldier had left Iran. This produced the Soviet outcry that the Americans were claiming to know better than the Iranian government how to protect the interests of Iran.[61]

The Red Army, however, began to evacuate Iran, and the Iranian government initiated talks with the leaders of the Azerbaijan regime.

Whereas Qavam intended to establish Iran's sovereignty over Azerbaijan gradually, the Shah wanted to take a more direct approach and dispatch troops immediately. Disagreements over tactics deepened the Shah's misgivings about Qavam's intentions. In May 1946, when George Allen replaced the ailing Wallace Murray as the American ambassador in Tehran, the "Shah vs. Qavam" dilemma awaited him. In a report to Washington, Allen stated that the Shah's policy was more likely to produce bloodshed than Qavam's but that the latter's conciliatory attitude might result in the continued existence of the Azerbaijan army. If dealing with the Azerbaijan delegation became impossible, Allen concluded, it was likely that Qavam would move in the direction of the Shah's position.[62]

On May 21, the government of Iran revealed that an inspection committee sent to Azerbaijan had found no evidence of Soviet troops. TASS reported on May 24 that evacuation of all Soviet troops from Iran was "official." But again, Secretary Byrnes refused to drop the matter from the UN agenda and instructed the American representative, Stettinius, to argue that the presence of Soviet troops was only one of the issues of dispute between Iran and the Soviet Union.[63] Perhaps Byrnes's attitude is best understood through his perception of the Soviet mentality, particularly that of his counterpart, Molotov. In *Speaking Frankly*, Byrnes wrote, "I have often thought that dealing with Mr. Molotov would be good experience for an attorney, who represents a corporation constantly being sued for damages, whose task is to play for time in the hope that the complainant will get tired of waiting for a trial and settle for a small part of his claim."[64] In retrospect, it appears that Mr. Byrnes favored keeping the issue on trial until the Soviets relinquished their entire claim with regard to Iran.

As did American efforts in the UN, the President's Army Day address on April 6 went a long way toward expressing the global nature of American concerns. Before a large crowd at Soldiers Field in Chicago, Truman called for a unified military service and the extension of the Selective Service Act, and he pledged American military might to the service of the United Nations. In regard to the Middle East, the President expressed American determination to protect the weak nations of the region and to extend economic aid. "We shall help," Truman declared, "because economic distress, anywhere in the world, is a fertile breeding ground for violent political upheaval."[65] A similar theme was echoed by Dean Acheson on June 4, in a speech before the Associated Harvard

Clubs in Boston. Acheson told the audience that the most important task in conducting foreign policy was to focus the will of the American people on problems beyond their shores. In Acheson's words, "the slogans 'Bring the boys home' and 'Don't be Santa Claus' are not among our more gifted or thoughtful contributions to the creation of a free and tranquil world."[66]

The increasingly assertive expressions of American global interests were welcomed by the Qavam government, which was seeking American support in dealing with the Azerbaijan crisis and the related issues of Soviet demands for oil concessions. Despite an announcement on June 13 that an understanding was reached with the Tabriz regime, Qavam was becoming convinced that the use of force was the only means of regaining Azerbaijan. In dealing with the problem of oil concessions, which required the approval of a new Majlis, Qavam first tried to widen his political base by incorporating various factions, including the Tudeh (Communist) members. In concert with this aim, and as a counterweight to the "Democrats of Azerbaijan," Qavam created his own "Democratic party of Iran."[67] Qavam planned either to ensure the election of a Majlis he could control, or, by including the opposition within the government and by appealing to their patriotism, to persuade them to reject the Soviet demands. But the unshakable loyalty of Tudeh members to Moscow, and the disapproval of the American ambassador and the Shah, finally persuaded Qavam to abandon this plan altogether. Henceforth, Qavam resorted to delaying the elections by arguing that the formation of a Majlis that represented the entire country required the control of Azerbaijan by the central government.

The revolt of tribes in southern Iran added a new twist to the prevailing political chaos. In late September, the Iranian government informed the State Department that there was conclusive evidence of British complicity in the matter and threatened to complain to "international authority." Allegedly, the British wanted to force the Iranian government to accept the old idea of giving them complete control of the southern oil fields while conceding the north to the Soviets. A similar impression was gathered by the American ambassador in Tehran. In a dispatch to Washington, George Allen stated that the British ambassador had complained that Tehran's continued perception of Azerbaijan as a part of Iran would lead to a "mushy" condition in which there was no clear-cut frontier, and that it would allow the Soviets to infiltrate into Iran and exert pressure southward. The British ambassador seemed to be indicating that "it would be preferable to cut off rotten part of the apple rather than let it infect the remainder."[68] Allen did not agree with this analysis, nor did the State Department, and, as later became clear, the opinion belonged solely to the British ambassador, as the Foreign Office categorically denied ever entertaining the idea.

The State Department, nevertheless, did include the possibility of an Anglo-Russian division of Iran in a series of questions submitted for the consideration of the Joint Chiefs of Staff (JCS). The JCS recommendation of October 12, 1946, stated that the division of Iran into Soviet and British spheres of domination was incongruent with American interests and suggested that "the United States should accede to Iranian requests for non-aggression items of military material, in reasonable amounts, to enable the Iranian government to maintain internal security."[69]

By mid-November, Qavam had decided to send troops to Azerbaijan. The rumors of Qavam's decision brought yet another Soviet threat against his government. On November 29, Qavam told the American ambassador that despite the Soviet threat he was determined to take military action, and he urgently asked for American support. The United States' position was communicated by Dean Acheson to the American ambassador in Tehran in a statement that imparted all the flavor of what later became known as the Truman Doctrine:

> You can assure Qavam that this Government will give its unqualified support to Iran or to any other power the integrity and independence of which may be threatened by external forces, provided that power shows courage and determination to maintain its own independence and freedom of action and provided it is willing to make its position clear to the world.[70]

Qavam was elated by the expression of the United States' support and told the American ambassador that Iran was willing to accept such responsibility. In a report to the Security Council on December 6, Hussein Ala, Iran's ambassador in Washington, explained that, in order to assure that election procedures were duly followed, the government of Iran was dispatching troops to Azerbaijan. Ala went on to state that, since the Soviet government had given "friendly admonition" that the movement of Iranian troops might cause disturbances, the Iranian government decided to inform the UN in advance so that the council would be in a better position to interpret the course of events.[71]

Ala's report, which had been prepared with the cooperation of the State Department and the Iranian authorities, accomplished several goals. First, it presented Iran's military action in Azerbaijan as rescuing the due process of election. Second, it informed the Security Council of the latest Soviet threat against Iran, though calling it "friendly admonition." Third, and most important, it facilitated the possibility of the United States' intervention under the auspices of the UN.

The Soviets were furious and chose to direct their anger at Qavam. The Russian ambassador demanded to know why Qavam had reported the Soviets' "friendly advice" to the Security Council. The manner in which the advice was given, Qavam explained, made it a threat. This explanation was not acceptable to the angry ambassador, who repeated the previous warning and told Qavam that if Iranian troops were sent to Azerbaijan the Soviet government "will have to revise its attitude toward you personally."[72]

Qavam, the sly old bird, as the British called him, seemed to draw strength from the latest round of Soviet threats. The frenzy of Soviet conduct indicated weakness, embarrassment, and inadequate preparation, all of which pleased Qavam. That the Soviets and their puppet regime in Azerbaijan were ill-prepared was demonstrated by the relative ease with which the Iranian army marched on Tabriz on December 11, 1946, and brought down the Azerbaijan regime exactly a year and a day after it was founded. Similarly, the other rebel regime, in Kurdistan, collapsed easily. Everyone, including Qavam, the American ambassador, and the Shah, was stunned by the rapid success of the Iranian army. But the return of the Iranian provinces was as real as the American role in making it possible. In describing the jubilant mood in Azerbaijan, the American Council in Tabriz reported to Washington, "At the sight of my car with American flag people cheered and applauded and shouted long live America."[73]

Why did the insurgent regimes crumble without any significant resistance? Why did the Soviets shy away from military involvement? The explanations advanced by both diplomats and scholars pointed to the lack of preparedness of the rebel regimes, and the failure of the Soviet Union to furnish them with heavy armaments. Soviet concern regarding the reaction of the Security Council, and the speed at which the insurgent regimes crumbled, precluded the possibility of Soviet

President Truman greets the Shah of Iran at the White House. November 1949.

military participation. The general consensus, however, was that the Soviets were finally convinced that the United States was not bluffing and would become directly involved if Iran were attacked by the Red Army.[74]

Whatever the Soviet plan may have been in Iran, it suffered a serious setback at the end of 1946. The Soviets' humiliation was compounded a few months later when the Iranian Majlis refused to ratify a previously promised oil concession. Above all, Azerbaijan became the first example of Soviet failure to maintain a puppet regime after it was established under the protection of the Red Army. As history was to demonstrate, compared to Soviet successes in other occupied territories, this was indeed a rare phenomenon.

The success of the Truman administration in Iran was due in no small measure to the cooperation of the British and the courage of the Iranian leaders. The British not only supported the American policies, but they also placed their vast experience and knowledge of Russian tactics at the disposal of the United States government. The Iranian leaders, for their part, demonstrated skill in dealing with the crisis and had the courage to risk facing the Red Army while more powerful countries were submitting to Soviet domination.

In retrospect, the resolution of the 1946 crisis in Iran proved to be one of the most successful tests of the American strategy of containment. Beyond checking Soviet advances, what distinguished the whole affair was the method by which the Truman administration confronted the Soviets. Although the limits of American tolerance were made clear to Stalin, the United States continued to appeal to the moral and legal principles of the UN charter. Unlike later examples of containment, this time the United States did not dispatch troops to do the fighting for the native inhabitants, nor was there covert interference in the political development of another country. Instead, the United States provided moral support and permitted the indigenous forces in Iran to defend the territorial integrity of their homeland. In brief, this was a case that even those who adhere to the so-called Third World viewpoint would be hard-pressed not to admire.

5

The Secret Side of Containment

> Finally we must have courage and self-confidence to cling to our own methods and conceptions of human society. After all, the greatest danger that can befall us in coping with this problem of Soviet communism, is that we shall allow ourselves to become like those with whom we are coping.[1]

The advice was offered in 1946, at the conclusion of a six-thousand-word telegram from the American chargé d'affaires in Moscow. The telegram, essentially a psychoanalysis of Soviet behavior, was praised by high officials of the United States government, and its author, George Kennan, was granted the status of a great strategist of the Cold War. As Kennan himself later acknowledged, it was not so much the objective reality as it was the subjective readiness of Washington officialdom that gave his report its special significance.[2] But the same subjective readiness that welcomed Kennan's report persuaded the American government to wage war against Communism even if that meant overlooking Kennan's concluding advice. What facilitated such conduct was the rising cost of containing Communism and the belief that America had no choice but to employ every available means.

When President Truman went before Congress in March 1947 to announce what became known as the Truman Doctrine, the cost was $400 million to aid Greece and Turkey. This amount, compared to the cost of saving Iran in 1946, was staggering but still acceptable. America was buying more than protection for Greece and Turkey; it was also advertising that the United States was committed to defending weaker nations in the name of Wilsonian self-determination. Similarly, when Congress approved the Marshall Plan in 1948, there was little doubt that the benefits would outweigh the costs. Therefore, at least in the early stages of containment, it seemed that the United States had both the moral commitment and the ability to afford the requirements of confronting the threat of global Communism.

There were, however, some early apprehensions regarding the logic and the future implications of the Truman Doctrine. One dissenting view was expressed by James Byrnes, who was Secretary of State until January 7, 1947. Byrnes considered the disturbing implication that the United States "would oppose the efforts of Communists in any country to gain control of the government, even when they acted without the interference of a foreign government and through the free votes of their own people." This policy was unacceptable to an old-school gentleman like Byrnes, who suggested "that was not and should never be the position of our government."[3] In 1947 a lively debate was ignited by the publication of "The Sources of Soviet Conduct" in the summer issue of *Foreign Affairs.* The revelation that the author, Mr. X, was none other than George Kennan gave the article the character of an official policy pronouncement and provoked Walter Lippmann to challenge Kennan's views. Unrestrained adherence to containment, Lippmann argued, was a "strategic monstrosity" that would foster commitments beyond American means and would result in complete national frustration.[4]

Despite such dissenting views, a Cold War consensus was achieved in the United States, primarily because the American people were informed that in a few years of peace the Soviet Union had overrun more territory by political subversion than the Red Army had conquered during the entire war. Moreover, the American people were sold on the idea that Truman's method in confronting the Soviets was the best. This fact became clear during the presidential election of 1948. The Republican candidate, Thomas Dewey, who promised to execute containment more effectively than Truman had, and the third-party candidate, Henry Wallace, who criticized Truman's tough approach, were both defeated at the polls.

Truman's honeymoon with his strategy of containment, however, proved to be short-lived. The Communist takeover in China in 1949 bred a new wave of discontent with American policies. The Republicans blamed the loss of China on the Truman administration, and Senator Joseph McCarthy accused the State Department of giving away China to the Communists. As the debate over China was still raging, North Korea invaded the South, in June 1950. The North Korean army, equipped with Russian-made weapons, including more than one hundred Russian-built tanks, crossed the 38th parallel with the purpose of bringing all Korea under Communist rule. By June 26, two days after the attack, President Truman had already committed American air and naval forces to the war. The mandate for a crusade for American action was furnished by the passage on June 27 of a UN Security Council resolution that called upon UN members to assist South Korea in repelling the armed aggression.

The early result of the war was a resounding victory for the UN forces, 90 percent of which were American and South Korean troops. But the euphoria of victory vanished when the Chinese entered the war with massive forces on October 26, driving the UN forces southward to the line that originally divided Korea. Truman was faced with difficult choices. The commander of the American army, General Douglas MacArthur, wanted to wage an all-out war against China. Others in the administration were concerned that a massive military campaign in Asia would expose Europe to a Soviet threat. The frustration that Walter Lippmann had warned about in 1947 was now beginning to emerge.

Against this background, Truman decided that the undeclared war in Korea was a "police action" and should remain a limited war. Truman's decision to dismiss General MacArthur from his post was unpopular and invited vitriolic attacks upon the administration. The public-approval ratings of the administration dropped to less than 30 percent, and Truman and Acheson were burned in effigy. Senator Richard Nixon described MacArthur's dismissal as "appeasement of Communism," and Senator Jenner of Indiana charged, "This country today is in the hands of a secret inner coterie which is directed by agents of the Soviet Union. . . . Our only course is to impeach President Truman and find out who is the secret invisible government which has so cleverly led our country down the road to destruction." And not to be outdone by others, Senator McCarthy declared that President Truman was a "son-of-a-bitch."[5]

General MacArthur was given a hero's welcome in the United States. Upon their arrival in San Francisco, the general and his wife paraded by car fourteen miles in two hours to their hotel. When the general went to Washington and delivered his farewell address before Congress, there was an emotional scene. A distinguished senator expressed fear for the safety of American institutions if MacArthur's speech had lasted much longer. Former president Herbert Hoover saw "reincarnation of St. Paul into a great General of the Army." And to top it all, Harvard-educated congressman Dewey Short proclaimed, "We saw a great hunk of God in the flesh, and we heard the voice of God."[6] Despite such displays, however, MacArthur was permitted to fade away as truce negotiations began in Korea.

The public outrage over MacArthur's dismissal, though indicative of America's proclivity toward hero worship, was in essence a symbol of rejecting limited war as a method of containment. Because Korea was the first war since the War of 1812 in which America failed to achieve a complete military victory, there was discontent with Truman's policies. The American public could not comprehend Truman's reluctance to employ all military means in a war that was taking American lives and undermining American prestige. The administration's failure to convince the American public of the necessity of limited war in Korea pushed Truman out of the White House just as some years later the experience of another limited war (Vietnam) cost Johnson the presidency of the United States.

Although it appeared that the Communist attack on South Korea caught Washington by surprise, there were indications that even before the attack the Truman administration was seriously concerned with the growing disparity between American military capabilities and the requirements of global involvements. In April 1950, shortly before the outbreak of the Korean War, President Truman had approved the recommendations put forward by National Security Council Document No. 68. This document, fully equipped with declamatory statements, was a prescription for bringing American power into balance with expanding commitments. The Korean War helped to launch NSC 68, which among other things had advocated using "any means" to promote revolt in Soviet-controlled countries and to "foster the seeds of destruction within the Soviet system." As an anti-Communist Manifesto, the spirit of NSC 68 was to survive long after the Truman administration had left office.

The legacy of the Truman administration also included the development of a new machinery for employing a cheap method of reducing the cost of containment. The method was covert operations, and the machinery was the Central Intelligence Agency. The story of the CIA is too important to be ignored or viewed with a childlike fascination with spies. At bottom, and for better or worse, the activities of the CIA have altered the destinies of some nations and touched the lives of their citizens, often without their knowledge and always without their consent. This is portrayed by the loving critics of the CIA, often implicitly, as clever and responsible, and by the unloving critics, often explicitly, as chilling and irresponsible. Others have come to regard it as being neither good nor bad, yet necessary for the protection of American interests abroad. Most, however, have preferred not to discuss the conduct of the CIA and either ignore the topic altogether or make only passing references to it in their writings. But the fact remains that without addressing the role of the CIA any analysis of postwar American involvement in world affairs is incomplete and at times even incomprehensible.

THE EMERGENCE OF THE CIA

The idea of a postwar intelligence agency was conceived by General William Donovan, the director of the Office of Strategic Services (OSS).[7] Before the war ended, Donovan utilized his access to President Roosevelt to present the blueprint for America's future intelligence agency. Roosevelt accepted the recommendation and drafted an executive order to that effect.[8] But the plan failed to materialize, principally because of interference from J. Edgar Hoover, the director of the Federal Bureau of Investigation.

The Hoover-Donovan feud was a pervasive feature of the American intelligence network during the war. In 1942, when Donovan's men had broken into the Spanish Embassy in Washington and were taking photographs of documents, two FBI squad cars suddenly pulled up outside the embassy and turned on their sirens. Donovan's agents fled.

Donovan complained to the President. But Roosevelt decided that the territory belonged to Hoover, and the embassy infiltration project was turned over to the FBI. Consequently, the President was persuaded to designate specific territories for Donovan and Hoover. The OSS received Europe and Asia, while the FBI was given North, Central, and South America.[9] Later, in order to stop Donovan's plan for establishing a postwar intelligence organization, Hoover somehow acquired a copy of Donovan's top-secret memorandum to the president and leaked the information to the anti-Roosevelt *Chicago Tribune.* The result was sensational reports by the *Tribune* that sparked a congressional uproar against the creation of an "American Gestapo" and that effectively halted Donovan's initiative.[10]

Following Roosevelt's death in April 1945, American intelligence operations received a more serious setback. President Truman, as part of an effort to reduce federal spending, declared that America had no use for a peacetime "Gestapo" and summarily disbanded the OSS by an executive order of September 20, 1945. But Truman's decision was short-lived. In January 1946, another presidential directive ordered the establishment of the Central Intelligence Group (CIG). The CIG proved to be ineffective, however, because of its reliance upon the War, Navy, and State departments for personnel and budget. By 1947 it became abundantly clear that sweeping changes were required. A new and most ambitious period in the life of American intelligence operations was about to begin.

The passage of the National Security Act in July 1947 provided for an independent Army, Navy, and Air Force coordinated by a Joint Chiefs of Staff under the authority of a Department of Defense. The legislation also provided for the establishment of the National Security Council (NSC) and changed the CIG to the Central Intelligence Agency (CIA). The tasks assigned to the CIA were vague. Among them was "duties related to intelligence affecting the national security as the NSC will from time to time direct."[11] The vagueness of the CIA's assignment was deliberate, for neither the executive nor the legislative branch of the American government was willing to be associated with the covert operations of the CIA. But as events were to testify, there was little inhibition against ordering the CIA to undo covertly what the policy-makers had been unable to prevent overtly.

At its very first meeting, the NSC decided to use the CIA as an active tool in the Cold War. A directive known as NSC 4/A ordered the CIA to undertake a broad range of covert activities to prevent a Communist victory in the upcoming Italian election.[12] The NSC decision stemmed from fear that if Communists won in Italy by popular vote all of Western Europe would follow suit. Dean Acheson, the Assistant Secretary of State, spoke of rotten apples infecting the whole barrel.[13] George Kennan, the head of the State Department Policy Planning Staff in March 1948, went beyond expressing concern and recommended outright American military action if the Communists won the election. The military supplies and technical advice given to the Italian military indicated that neither the Truman administration nor the Italian government was prepared to accept an election defeat as final, and that an anti-Communist coup would have followed a failure at the polls.[14]

In light of the perceived threat to American interests in Europe, Truman decided to accept the NSC recommendation and authorized the CIA to contribute about one million dollars to the Christian Democratic Party. When they won the election of April 1948, the CIA took the credit.[15] In the words of historians Stephen E. Ambrose and Richard H. Immerman: "What a bargain! For a paltry million dollars, Italy and Western Europe were saved. Or so at least the CIA could and did argue. It was a cautious, conservative venture into covert ops, but it was a start."[16]

In May 1948, Kennan recommended the creation of a permanent task force to do for the world what the special operation had done for Italy. On June 18, 1948, six days before the Soviet blockade of Berlin, the National Security Council superseded NSC 4/A with a new directive, NSC 10/2, authorizing the creation of a covert-action organization with the typically euphemistic name of the Office of Policy Coordination (OPC). According to NSC 10/2, the mandate of this new organization was to indulge in activities related to "propaganda, economic warfare, preventive direct action, including sabotage, anti-sabotage, demolition and evacuation measures; subversion against hostile states, including assistance to underground resistance groups, and support of indigenous anti-Communist elements in threatened countries of the free world." Such activities had to be "so planned and conducted that any U.S. government responsibility for them is not evident to unauthorized persons and that if uncovered the U.S. Government can plausibly disclaim any responsibility for them."[17]

In the following year, 1949, the CIA was given congressional approval by the passage of the Central Intelligence Agency Act. This legislation exempted the CIA from all federal laws requiring the disclosure of number of employees, their names, their functions, and their salaries. The CIA director was granted the power to spend money "without regard to the provisions of law and regulations relating to the expenditure of government funds.... such expenditure to be accounted for solely on the certificate of the director."[18] Thus, the making of an invisible government within the United States government was well underway.

With its basic structure in place, the CIA began attracting a cast of characters to run its operations. Some were old faces from the OSS, and others were young college graduates, whose enthusiasm often exceeded their ability. Thomas Powers, in his extensively researched book, has described three distinct CIA personalities: the spy runners, the analysts, and the covert operators. Richard Helms was a classic example of the first personality, a man with discretion, restraint, and an equal enthusiasm for both the penetration and preservation of secrets. The second personality type was the analyst, who had an insatiable appetite for anything that could be written down, stacked on a desk, and read, including newspapers, charts of radio traffic, telephone directories, railroad timetables, and so on. Unlike spies, who were obsessed with missing pieces, the analysts were devoted to patterns. Whereas spies were haunted by the possibility that the missing piece might explain it all, the analysts were convinced that the pattern would bridge the gap. Two basic assumptions of the CIA analysts were that the best clue to the future was past behavior and that nations did not take risks unless there was a substantial chance of success. In short, the analysts believed that nations were both rational and consistent.[19]

The third personality type was the covert operator—men like Kermit Roosevelt, Frank Wisner, Richard Bissell, Desmond Fitzgerald, Mike Burke, and Tracy Barnes. In describing these men, Powers wrote:

> All were gregarious, intrigued by possibilities, liked to do things, had three bright ideas a day, shared the optimism of stock market plungers, and were convinced that every problem had its handle, and that the CIA could find a way to reach it. They also tended to be white Anglo-Saxon patricians from old families with old money, at least in the beginning, and they somehow inherited traditional British attitudes toward the colored races of the world—not the pukka sahib arrogance of the Indian Raj, but the mixed fascination and condescension of men like T. E. Lawrence, who were enthusiastic partisans of the alien cultures into

which they dipped for a time and rarely doubted their ability to help, until it was too late.... [20]

Differences among the CIA personality types notwithstanding, they seemed quite capable of joining forces when the agency was threatened by Senator McCarthy's witch-hunt in the early 1950s. McCarthy had indicated that, when he had finished finding the Communists in the State Department, the next target would be the CIA. In response, President Truman in 1950 appointed General Walter Bedell Smith, the former ambassador to the Soviet Union, as the director of the CIA. Smith was an able administrator and had the reputation of being a right-wing military man who looked for Communists under his bed at night. "I know you won't believe this," an ex-CIA agent later confided, "but Smith once warned Eisenhower that [Nelson] Rockefeller was a Communist." Despite Smith's reputation, however, Senator McCarthy and his friends were unwilling to spare the CIA. It was the pressure of McCarthyites that compelled Smith in 1952 to tell a congressional committee: "I believe there are Communists in my own organization [the CIA]. I do everything I can to detect them, but I am morally certain, since you are asking the question, that they are there."[21]

Whether Smith was buying time or planning to hand over the CIA to McCarthy is not quite clear. What is clear, however, is that the man who saved the CIA from McCarthy's madness was not director Smith, but deputy director Allen Dulles. Because of his personal makeup, family background, education, and experiences in intelligence work and in teaching, Allen Dulles was simply too secure to be intimidated by the likes of Joseph McCarthy. In contrast to his own brother, John Foster Dulles—who had disappointed the Foreign Service officers by failing to protect the State Department—Allen Dulles was admired by the CIA employees because he had the courage to stand up to McCarthy's gang, whom Dean Acheson had referred to as "the primitives."

Allen Dulles told a meeting of six hundred CIA officers that they would be protected against McCarthy, that no CIA officer would be forced to testify before McCarthy's Senate committee, and that there would be an immediate dismissal of any CIA employee who broke ranks and talked to McCarthy's gang. In addition, Dulles assigned Lyman Kirkpatrick to oversee the CIA's own internal investigation, and he asked Richard Helms to form a committee to counter McCarthyite attempts to infiltrate the CIA and frame CIA employees. The Helms

Allen Dulles appearing before the Senate Armed Services Committee that recommended his confirmation as director of the Central Intelligence Agency. Washington, D.C., February 19, 1953. (Source: Harris & Ewing)

committee was successful in keeping an eye on McCarthy's activities, thereby allowing the CIA to be one step ahead of the game.[22] In brief, because of the determination of Allen Dulles and the cooperation of the CIA officers, the agency not only survived McCarthyism but actually gathered strength from the experience.

During the same period, CIA capabilities, particularly in regard to covert operations, were greatly enhanced. As disclosed years later, the number of personnel of OPC (the covert arm of the CIA) jumped from 302 in 1949 to 2,812 in 1952. Also added were 3,142 overseas contract personnel. The OPC had seven foreign stations in 1949, but by 1952 there were forty-seven such stations. The budget for OPC skyrocketed from $4.7 million in 1949 to $82 million by 1952.[23]

The expansion of CIA programs reflected a growing concern with the Communist threat. Whereas the Korean conflict demonstrated the military and political difficulties associated with fighting Communism abroad, McCarthyism proved the absurdity of a witch-hunt at home. Therefore, it appeared that the less costly alternative was to leave foreign enemies to the CIA and to let the FBI deal with the domestic ones. Of course, this meant that both agencies were invariably granted latitude in deciding America's friends and foes. The general story of Hoover's FBI is fairly well known. As for the CIA, it was to become what Allen Dulles himself referred to as "the State Department for unfriendly countries."

An intriguing aspect of the CIA's influence on American diplomacy is related to the extent to which the CIA itself was influenced by the intelligence agencies of other friendly governments. Starting with the Second World War, the work of American intelligence and counterintelligence was largely dependent on liaisons with foreign intelligence services. In fact, until the 1960s, as much as 70 percent of the CIA's information was collected by foreign intelligence, particularly by the British. Richard Helms, later a director of the CIA, was most uncomfortable with the primacy of foreign intelligence services, especially that of the British, who had made it clear that they ought to run all the spies while the Americans provided all the money.[24] Another CIA personality, Kermit Roosevelt, who was in charge of the operation to overthrow the government of Iran in 1953, also acknowledged the contributions of the British. Mr. Roosevelt, without expressing resentment toward the British for the role they played, confided that they had indeed contributed intelligence that had influenced the CIA operation in Iran.[25] There is no conclusive evidence, however, that British agents deliberately misinformed their American counterparts to provoke American action against selective targets.

Generally speaking, it is difficult to determine to what extent friendly foreign governments have influenced American policies by ordering their spies to transmit self-serving but otherwise inaccurate information to the CIA. Even if the origin of a given CIA estimate is traced back to some foreign intelligence source, there is still no certainty as to what role, if any, the information plays in shaping United States policies, because the select individual or individuals who are in a position to know the nature and logic of foreign policy decisions usually have little incentive to reveal them. The fear of admitting the truth to their constituency and an obsession with their personal image in history may compel political figures either to delete embarrassing facts from their statements and memoirs or to present them in the camouflage of universal humanitarian ideals. The result is the ambiguity that often surrounds the logic of foreign policy decisions, at least in the opinion of historians who are disinclined to accept official explanations at face value. If such ambiguity is acknowledged, then it also relates to the role of the CIA. That is why pointing to the CIA as having fostered certain decisions may leave out more than it includes.

The habit of using the CIA and then blaming the agency for misconduct has become part of the folklore of American diplomacy. President Truman, the man who had authorized the creation of the CIA, and among other things had asked the agency to interfere in the Italian election of 1948, told a syndicated newspaper interviewer in 1963:

> I never had any thought that when I set up the CIA that it would be injected into peacetime cloak-and-dagger operations. Some of the complications and embarrassment that I think we have experienced are in part attributable to the fact that this quiet intelligence arm of the President has been removed from its intended role [and] that it is being interpreted as a symbol of sinister and mysterious foreign intrigue—and a subject for Cold War enemy propaganda.[26]

George Kennan, one of the original promoters of a permanent covert task force, expressed his disapproval of the CIA in 1975. Kennan suggested that he thought such a task force "would be a facility which could be used when and if an occasion arose when it might be needed. There might be years when we wouldn't have to do anything like this. But if the occasion arose, we wanted somebody in the Government who would have the funds, the experience, the expertise to do these things and to do them in a proper way." Apparently, the frequency of the CIA's covert activities and the manner in which the CIA did "these things" displeased Mr. Kennan, who declared, "It did not work out at all the way I had conceived it. . . . "[27]

Whatever the merits of such statements, the fact remains that the creation of the CIA was authorized by President Truman in 1947, and the establishment of its permanent covert task force was suggested in 1948 by Mr. Kennan, who was then the head of the State Department's Policy Planning Staff. During the Truman administration, the CIA was fully developed to become involved in worldwide covert operations. As noted in a report of the Congressional Select Committee on Intelligence Activities, "by 1953 the Agency had achieved the basic structure and scale it retained for the next twenty years."[28]

The CIA has also received periodic admonishment from the members of the legislative branch of the American government. Having survived

McCarthy's brand of conservatism in the 1950s, the CIA was attacked by Senator Frank Church and other liberals in the 1970s. In the aftermath of Watergate, when criticism of the CIA was fashionable, the agency was regarded as something of a delinquent orphan. Richard Helms, already accused by Nixon's White House of not being enough of a team player, was made to leave his post as ambassador in Iran to come to Washington, where he was subjected to harsh criticism by some members of Congress who acted as if they had just discovered that the CIA was not the Boy Scouts of America. To Helms's credit, he was able to handle the entire charade with utmost restraint, for any serious attempt to defend himself and the agency would have amounted to telling the whole world that playing dirty tricks was implicit in the mandate given to the CIA and that more often than not the CIA's covert operations were specifically requested by the NSC and approved by the president of the United States.

In the final analysis, the role of the CIA in American foreign policy should neither be ignored nor studied with a prosecutorial approach. For all intents and purposes, the CIA is usually assigned what the White House considers to be the terminal cases—the ones that have not responded to conventional means. Whereas the agency must usually savor its successes in silence, a failure often awakens the self-righteous spirit of some individuals in the executive and legislative branches of American government. The important fact to consider in judging the CIA, however, is that the conduct of the agency is not the cause but a symptom of what is right or wrong with the American perception of world affairs.

EISENHOWER, DULLES, AND THE NEW LOOK

The euphoria of winning the Second World War, the buoyant optimism that once had compelled Dean Acheson to call America the only nation capable of grabbing hold of history, and the daring confidence implicit in declaring the Truman Doctrine were all fading when Eisenhower assumed the presidency of the United States in 1953. The suspicion and hysteria of McCarthy's era and the rising cost of carrying commitments abroad had taken their toll and had brought into question the viability of American foreign policy. Containment was no longer the easy game it once had appeared. There were no more Cinderella stories such as Iran in 1946 and Greece and Turkey in 1947. The shock had come in 1949 when the Communists took over China and when the Soviets eliminated the American nuclear monopoly. Then, in 1950, North Korea attacked the South, compelling the United States to face the first painful test of containment by limited war. It appeared that America was made to react to events and pay an unacceptable price in the process. Therefore, some changes in strategy were clearly needed, even if that meant giving a new look to the old · ways.

Was it conceivable that America's very success in the immediate postwar years had produced an inability to adjust to qualitative changes in the international system? Was it possible that Truman's very attempt to make America's posture clear to the world had resulted in predictability? Was the Soviet Union exploiting these vulnerabilities to pick the place and the time to confront the United States? Answers to such questions were judged to be affirmative by Eisenhower and Dulles, who sought to inject a note of deliberate ambiguity into American foreign policy.[29]

At the heart of the new ambiguity was the threat of "massive retaliation" against targets of American choosing. Eisenhower thought that with this policy "no one would undertake to say exactly what we would do under a variety of circumstances."[30] To further the ambiguity, it was advertised that "containment" was negative and immoral and that it should be supplanted by "liberation," which presumably meant the United States would take the initiative to liberate the "captive peoples" of Communist countries. But as later became clear, the aim of the American crusade was confined neither to Communist-controlled countries nor to those immediately threatened by Communism; it also included every nation that possessed the potential to become a liability in the American-Soviet struggle for power and influence.

The introduction of the "new look" was as much the result of the widening interest-power gap as it was related to the perceptions of its two principle architects—President Eisenhower and Secretary of State John Foster Dulles. These men, unlike some recent American leaders, had not stumbled into places of power but had come well prepared to assume the role of leadership. Behind the exterior of their public image—which usually portrayed a smiling Eisenhower teeing off at some golf course while the grim Dulles dealt with the serious stuff—they were men who had firm convictions as to how the world must be managed.

Eisenhower, the war hero, could be soft without being accused of appeasing America's enemies. Eisenhower never doubted who was in charge and had the knack of delegating authority without surrendering control. He had the ability to overcome the passion of the moment in the interest of better judgment. His conviction that things were not as they appeared was revealed by the statement, "Behind every human action, the truth may be hidden.... Unless circumstances and responsibility demanded an instant judgment, I learned to reserve mine until the last proper moment."[31] In the words of historian Robert Divine, "What some perceived as excessive caution and even indecision would prove in time to be admirable qualities of patience and prudence that enabled Eisenhower to deal effectively with many of the international crises of the 1950s."[32]

By contrast, Dulles played the role of an enforcer of law and morality. He was allowed to deliver the moralistic rhetoric, to ward off right-wing Republicans, and to absorb the criticism from the liberals. Dulles was particularly suited for this role because of his temperament and his constant fear of not sounding tough enough. As Eisenhower himself once lamented, "Foster is just too worried about being accused of sounding like Truman and Acheson."[33] But it was Winston Churchill who made the remark that "Foster Dulles is the only case I know of a bull who carries his china shop with him."[34]

In his zeal to show toughness, Dulles sometimes irritated his boss. "I don't think we can get much out of a Korean settlement," Dulles had said, "until we have shown—before all Asia—our clear superiority by giving the Chinese one hell of a licking." In response to this, Eisenhower had replied, "If Mr. Dulles and all his sophisticated advisors really mean that they can not talk peace seriously, then I am in the wrong pew. For if it's *war* we should be talking about, I *know* the people to give me advice on that—and they are not in the State Department. Now either we cut out all this fooling around and make a serious bid for peace—or we forget the whole thing."[35]

Despite their obvious differences, Eisenhower and Dulles worked effectively together. Their contrasting public images were for the most part carefully tailored to aid the aims of American diplomacy. Of course, there was nothing original about projecting the image of a bitter-sweet

Secretary of State John Foster Dulles. Washington, D.C., January 1953.

or good-bad combination of political actors. The method was well tested in the Old World and was later employed by Nixon and Kissinger with an ironic twist that depicted Nixon as the devious one while Kissinger attempted to sell the image of a decent intellectual. The contrast between Eisenhower and Dulles was by far more genuine, as were their respect and appreciation for each other.

The factor most responsible for Eisenhower-Dulles cooperation, however, was their common belief that history had imposed an obligation upon them to decide what was good for the rest of the world. This attitude was most pronounced when it concerned the destiny of Third World countries. Because of a deep suspicion of Third World nationalism, the Eisenhower administration came to view the emergence of nationalist movements as undermining the American crusade against Communism. Consequently, nationalist leaders such as Musaddiq of Iran, Arbenz of Guatemala, and Nasser of Egypt were regarded as "undesirables," not because they were Communists, but because their "neutralism" was perceived as being immoral and as helping the Communist devils. The issue then was not whether to remove the "undesirables" from power, but to find the most efficient way of achieving this goal.[36]

That Eisenhower and Dulles opted for the use of covert operations reflected both the rising cost of conventional means and the development of covert capabilities. Eisenhower's decision was reinforced by the report of a special investigative committee headed by the famous World War II aviator General James Doolittle. The President had appointed this committee and had welcomed its recommendations, which stated bluntly:

> It is now clear that we are facing an implacable enemy whose avowed objective is world domination by whatever means and at whatever cost. There are no rules in such a game. Hitherto acceptable norms of human conduct do not apply. If the United States is to survive, long-standing American concepts of "fair play" must be reconsidered. We must develop effective espionage and counterespionage services and must learn to subvert, sabotage, and destroy our enemies by more clever, more sophisticated, and more effective methods than those used against us. It may become necessary that the American people be made acquainted with, understand, and support this fundamentally repugnant philosophy.[37]

The chilling conclusion of the Doolittle report was a far cry from the advice offered by George Kennan in 1946. But the subjective readiness of Washington officialdom, which once had welcomed Kennan's long telegram, was now prepared to regard the Doolittle report as a viable prescription for American diplomacy.

6

Containment by Covert Operation: Iran 1953

James Lochridge, a thirty-seven-year-old American of medium build and height, handed his passport to a custom guard at Khaniquin, a border post on the Iran-Iraq frontier. It was July 19, 1953. The chances that the semiliterate guard would understand English were as remote as Khaniquin itself. With help from Mr. Lochridge, the guard focused on the page of the passport that listed the notable features of the holder. The guard then laboriously transcribed the name of the holder as "Mr. Scar on Right Forehead." This was considered a good omen by Mr. Lochridge, who had endeavored to keep his arrival in Iran a secret.

Although rather nondescript, Mr. Lochridge was no ordinary American. Before his departure from Washington, the highest American officials were concerned about his health because of the untimely development of a kidney stone. When it was decided that solving his medical problem took precedence over his mission, there was serious apprehension that Mr. Lochridge might utter something indiscreet while coming out of the anesthesia, and so a special nurse with top-secret clearance was assigned to look after him. Upon emerging from the anesthesia, he wanted to know what he had said. The nurse, sporting a mischievous look, assured him, "Nothing that betrayed any state secrets."

En route to Iran, Mr. Lochridge had picked up Francis Granger, a CIA operator stationed in Iraq as a member of the American diplomatic mission. The two of them had driven across Iraq to Khaniquin with the purpose of continuing on to Tehran, where Mr. Lochridge could rest and prepare for a clandestine meeting with the Shah of Iran.[1]

The Shah was told in advance of the possibility of such a meeting by his sister, Princess Ashraf, who had made a special trip from Switzerland to Iran for this purpose. This was a dangerous trip for the princess because Prime Minister Musaddiq regarded her as corrupt and dangerous and had compelled the Shah to send her abroad. To persuade the princess to return to Tehran, the CIA had selected a U.S. Air Force officer by the name of Charles Mason, who considered himself to be the greatest lady-killer of the twentieth century. Mason accepted the assignment with enthusiasm and, along with Britisher Gordon Somerset, approached the princess in Switzerland. Although there were various accounts of what transpired in Switzerland, the result was that the princess agreed to deliver the message personally to the Shah.[2]

Late in the evening of August 1, 1953, Mr. Lochridge slipped out of his hideout near Tehran and got into the back seat of a nondescript black sedan. Although the car was suitably non-royal, the driver was to take Mr. Lochridge to the Royal Palace. As they approached the palace gates, Mr. Lochridge huddled down on the floor of the car and pulled a blanket over himself. The guard at the gate waved the car through. Halfway between the gates and the palace, the driver parked the car and walked away. A slim figure approached the car. Mr. Lochridge pulled the blanket out of the way and elevated himself to the back seat as the slim man entered the car and sat beside him. The two men immediately recognized each other.

"Good evening, Mr. Roosevelt," said the slim man. "I cannot say that I expected to see you, but this is a pleasure."

"Good evening, Your Majesty. It is a long time since we met each other, and I am glad you recognize me. It may make establishing my credentials a bit easier."

The Shah laughed. "That will hardly be necessary. Your name and presence is all the guarantee I need."[3]

The Roosevelt—alias Lochridge—that the Shah met at midnight was

Princess Ashraf, the Shah's twin sister, on a visit to a European city. 1947.

Kermit (Kim) Roosevelt, the grandson of Theodore Roosevelt and the cousin of FDR. Kermit Roosevelt was a veteran of the OSS and later became the chief of the Middle East Department of the CIA. He was with the CIA at a time when the agency was still the domain of white Anglo-Saxon patricians from old families with old money. As described in Chapter 5, he was among the CIA personalities that "shared the optimism of stock market plungers, and were convinced that every problem had its handle, and that the CIA could find a way to reach it." As for his effectiveness, Kermit Roosevelt was once described as "the quiet American . . . the last person you would expect to be up to his neck in dirty tricks."[4]

As the Shah and Kermit Roosevelt continued their conversation in the car, Mr. Roosevelt explained that he was representing President Eisenhower and Prime Minister Churchill and that the American and British governments had devised "Operation Ajax" to overthrow the government of Dr. Musaddiq and to keep the Shah in power. To establish the authenticity of this plan, Mr. Roosevelt informed the Shah:

Kermit Roosevelt and the Shah of Iran at Sa'adabad Palace, north of Tehran. 1964. (Source: Christian Herter, Jr.)

> President Eisenhower will confirm this himself by a phrase in a speech he is about to deliver in San Francisco—actually within the next twenty-four hours. Prime Minister Churchill has arranged to have a specific change made in the time announcement on the BBC broadcast tomorrow night. Instead of saying "It is now midnight," the announcer will say, "It is now"—pause—"*exactly* midnight."[5]

With the preliminaries out of the way, both the Shah and Mr. Roosevelt were somewhat relaxed. The Shah was pleased with the expression of American and British support, and Mr. Roosevelt was relieved that the young monarch was calm and collected and otherwise aware of the delicacy of the situation. At dawn the meeting came to an end.

"Good night—or should I say good morning?—Mr. Roosevelt. I am glad to welcome you once again to my country."

"And I am very glad to be here, Your Majesty. I am full of confidence that our undertaking will succeed."

Kermit Roosevelt left the palace driveway in the same manner he had arrived. "Operation Ajax," the first major covert action approved by President Eisenhower, was underway.[6]

To explain the compelling interest that called for a Roosevelt to hide under a blanket, for Churchill to use the BBC for a personal message, and for Eisenhower to implant code signals in a speech, a review of the historical data is required. This review must deal with two distinct though interrelated features of the events of 1953. The first is the nature of the problem that the Eisenhower administration inherited. The second is the nature of the solution that Eisenhower was persuaded to accept. In evaluating each feature, it is imperative to consider the course of events as it was perceived by the political actors in 1953, and not as it appears in historical hindsight. Whatever the link between the events of 1953 and subsequent American-Iranian relations, it is still a separate subject and should be addressed accordingly.

THE PROBLEM EISENHOWER INHERITED

Shortly after Eisenhower's election in November of 1952, a representative of the American petroleum industry informed the President-elect that the situation in Iran was a "prairie fire which would spread throughout the Middle East to the detriment of American oil interests in other countries. We have good reason to believe that, unless a prompt solution is obtained to avoid Iran going to the Communists, the prairie fire of Communism will consume all the strategic interests of the United States and the West throughout the Middle East."[7] The villain who could cause such problems for America was identified as the prime minister of Iran, Dr. Musaddiq, who had endeavored to nationalize the Iranian oil industry in an attempt to end the British monopoly of Persian petroleum.

Although they described Musaddiq to Eisenhower as a Communist threat, the American oil companies and their British counterparts were concerned that Musaddiq's actions might set a precedent for other oil-producing countries to follow. In addition, if Iran had been allowed to sell her oil independently, it would have interfered with the industry's international market controls. But in presenting their case in the form of anti-Communism, the oil companies were assured of getting the attention of the President-elect, who subsequently—on the advice of

Secretary of State John Foster Dulles and the director of the CIA, Allen Dulles—became convinced that the situation in Iran must be viewed as a test of containment.

The problem facing President Eisenhower had a long history and had demanded the continuous attention of the Truman administration. The economic difficulties of Iran, the rise of Musaddiq as a nationalist leader, and Musaddiq's confrontation with the British and the Shah were all products of events shaped by Persian political culture and the struggle to control Iran's petroleum. The background necessary for understanding Persian political culture—its configuration of religion and politics, its early experience in dealing with the West, its fear of foreign powers, and its tendency to seek a new foreign power to counterbalance the influence of the old ones—has been discussed in Chapters 2 and 3. What remains to be addressed here is the link between Iranian oil and the rise of nationalism that was to produce the "prairie fire" described to Eisenhower.

The twists and turns of political events in contemporary Persia have been intimately associated with the story of Persian petroleum. Baron Julius de Reuter, a naturalized British subject, had managed in 1872 to acquire the rights to the entire mineral resources of Persia for a period of seventy years. In return, Reuter was to participate in Iran's economic development, including deciding what roads should be built and what rivers regulated. The decision of the Persian monarch to grant Reuter such rights was indeed a most extraordinary surrender of a nation's resources. There was some opposition within Iran to this concession, but more important, the Russians were infuriated that the Persian monarch had favored the British so blatantly. Primarily as a result of Russian pressure, the Shah was compelled to abrogate the concession in 1873. Although domestic opposition played a minor role in this affair, it was significant in that it revealed an early sign of modern nationalism in Iran.

Faced with a bankrupt treasury, Nasir al-Din Shah sought financial support by granting other forms of concessions. For example, Reuter was given permission in 1889 to establish the Imperial Bank of Persia, with the exclusive right to issue bank notes in Iran for a period of sixty years. And in 1890, another British subject, Major G. Talbot, was granted a concession that gave him the exclusive right to export Iranian tobacco and to sell tobacco products in Iran. The Shah was to receive £15,000 annually and one-quarter of the company's profits after the deduction of all business expenses and after the payments of dividends. Once again, the Russians were displeased, and there was discontent within Iran. But this time public discontent played the major role in shaping the events that not only caused the cancelation of the tobacco concession but that later were viewed as a unified expression of Iranian nationalism.

Public sentiment was articulated in a letter to the Shah from a religious leader, Hasan-i-Shirazi. The Shah first responded by taking away Talbot's right to sell tobacco within Iran. But Shirazi and his followers were not satisfied. Shirazi issued a fatwa (a legal opinion of the clergy) asking the public to abandon smoking until the concession was canceled. The public response was overwhelming. The Shah, as well as the British, was shocked by this response, and the Shah was forced to abrogate the concession. Talbot demanded £650,000 as indemnity from the Persian government and settled for £500,000. Because the Persian treasury could not pay this amount, the Shah had to borrow the money from the British Bank at 6 percent interest.[8]

Six years after granting the tobacco concession, Nasir al-Din Shah was assassinated, and his son, Muzaffar al-Din, assumed the role of sovereign. Like his predecessor, Muzaffar al-Din Shah looked for a simple way to acquire needed revenue. Petroleum still remained the lure for inviting foreign capital. William Knox D'Arcy, a British entrepreneur, became interested in reports of oil deposits in Iran and dispatched Alfred Marriott to negotiate a concession. The individual responsible for fostering an agreement, however, was Sir Arthur Hardinge, the British minister in Tehran, who arranged for a bribe to be paid to the Persian authorities to insure the most favorable deal. As a result, D'Arcy was granted a concession in 1901, after paying £20,000 to the Persian treasury and £25,000 in bribes to the Persian authorities, and agreeing to pay 16 percent of his net annual profit to the government of Iran.[9] Under this concession, D'Arcy was given a sixty-year right to all Persian oil resources except those in the five northern provinces. D'Arcy named his venture the First Exploitation Company. In 1908 oil was struck, and in 1909 the Anglo-Persian Oil Company (APOC) was formed. After the discovery of oil, however, the British government became deeply interested, and at the urging of Winston Churchill, then First Lord of the Admiralty, Great Britain purchased D'Arcy's shares in 1914 and acquired majority control in the APOC. The activities of the APOC—after 1935 called the Anglo-Iranian Oil Company (AIOC)—and its confrontation with the rise of nationalism in Iran were to become the single most important factor in shaping the contemporary history of Persia.[10]

The evolution of D'Arcy's concession into the APOC took place during an interesting period of Persian history. What had begun as a mild protest over Reuter's concession of 1872, then had developed into a unified opposition to Talbot's concession of 1880, finally became a major political movement in the aftermath of D'Arcy's concession. The lack of patriotism and competence on the part of the monarchs of the Qajar dynasty finally convinced the Persians that, instead of fighting individual concessions granted to foreigners, they ought to curb the power of the monarchs who granted such concessions to support their extravagant life-styles. Inspired by the European constitutional reforms of the nineteenth century, the Persians sought to reduce the power of the Shah. This movement, which became known as the Persian Revolution of 1906, compelled Muzaffar al-Din Shah to grant permission for the establishment of an assembly of public representatives (Majlis).[11] When the ailing Shah died in 1907, however, his successor undermined the constitution, and with Anglo-Russian blessings, he ordered his troops to attack the Majlis in 1908. But the action backfired, resulting in nationwide riots that forced Muhammad Ali Shah to abdicate in 1909, making his twelve-year-old son, Ahmad Mirza, the Shah of Persia.

Throughout this period, American policy advocated total abstention from interfering in Persian politics. It was not until 1911 that the United States agreed to send Morgan Shuster to serve as the financial advisor to the Persian government. Shuster's mission to Iran, and Millspaugh's mission eleven years later, were both requested by the Persian government. Similarly, it was at the request of Persian authorities that American oil companies became involved in Iran. That Iran invited American influence—as described in Chapters 2 and 3—was the result of America's anticolonial posture and Iran's desire to seek a third power to counter Anglo-Russian imperial rivalry.

The first American oil company that indicated interest in Persia was Standard Oil of New Jersey. In 1921 the company informed the Persian government that it was willing to accept a concession in northern Iran, which was excluded from the territory given to the APOC. But there were complications. To start with, a Tsarist Russian, Akaki Khoshtaria, had been granted a concession in northern Iran in 1916. After the

Russian Revolution, the British (APOC) negotiated with Khoshtaria, buying his concession in 1920 for £100,000. As far as the Persian and Russian authorities were concerned, however, all the agreements of the Tsarist period were invalid, including the concession given to Khoshtaria in 1916. In addition, the Russians had signed a treaty with Iran in 1921 that, among other things, had tied the annulment of concessions given to Tsarist Russia to a provision that forbade Iran to grant such concessions to a third party.

In order to pacify the British and the Soviets, the Persian authorities argued that the concession originally given to Khoshtaria had never been valid because it had not been ratified by the Majlis. On November 22, 1921, the Majlis unanimously approved granting Standard Oil of New Jersey a fifty-year concession with the stipulations that the concession was not transferable and that the company would pay Iran 15 percent of its gross revenue. But it immediately became clear that the British still held the winning card. The APOC contended that, according to the concession given to D'Arcy, it had exclusive rights to oil transportation in Iran. Consequently, Standard Oil was forced to make a deal with the British. In exchange for transportation rights, Standard Oil accepted joint participation with the APOC in northern Iran, forming the new Perso-American Petroleum Company.[12]

This development disturbed the Persian authorities, who had encouraged an American company's interest in Iran for the purpose of reducing the British monopoly of Persian petroleum. The Russians were also alarmed by the extension of British influence into northern Iran. If they were forced to choose, even the Russians would have preferred to see an American company instead of the British in northern Iran. As a consequence, the Persian government declared that the concession given to Standard Oil was invalid because the company had violated the provision that specifically forbade the transfer of this concession. However, the Majlis authorized the Persian government to seek a new agreement with Standard Oil or any other American company. The new effort produced a proposal from Sinclair Consolidated Oil Corporation in August of 1922. By then, the rise of Riza Khan—later Riza Shah and the founder of the Pahlavi dynasty—was changing the political picture of Iran by offering to impose order upon the prevailing state of anarchy. When the Persian government signed an agreement with Sinclair in December of 1923, Riza Khan, then Iran's prime minister, told the American chargé d'affaires, "We want to eradicate the economic dominance of Britain and Russia in Iran; and the signing of this concession with an American company will be the beginning of stronger ties between the United States and Iran."[13]

The Persian government had approved Sinclair's concession despite opposition from the British, who continued to claim the petroleum of northern Iran on the basis of having purchased Khoshtaria's concession of 1916. The APOC was also threatening to deny Sinclair transportation rights. To overcome this problem, Harry Sinclair began negotiating with the Russians to gain transportation rights through Russia to the Black Sea. In exchange for transportation rights, Sinclair promised the Russians to use his influence to secure the recognition of the Soviet Union by the United States. Apparently, Sinclair had discussed the issue with two of his friends, Secretary of the Interior Albert Fall and Attorney General Harry Dougherty. But when the Teapot Dome scandal erupted in 1924, implicating Sinclair and his friends, the possibility of a deal with the Russians fell through. In addition, financial difficulties and a glut on the American oil market persuaded Sinclair to abandon the concession in Persia.[14]

From 1925 to 1936 American oil companies abstained from seeking concessions in Iran. But petroleum continued to play a crucial role in Iran's political development. In 1925 the reign of the Qajar dynasty was officially ended, and the Majlis passed a constitutional amendment that made Riza Khan the Shah of Iran. Although Riza Shah gave priority to reducing the Anglo-Russian domination of Iran, his enthusiasm by far exceeded the military and economic power available to him. An outstanding example of Riza Shah's predicament was his confrontation with the APOC.

During 1931–32, the APOC paid markedly reduced royalties to the Persian government. Although the Depression was chiefly responsible for reduced oil revenues, the APOC was accused of shortchanging the Persian government. Riza Shah—who had earlier attempted to renegotiate with the APOC and had failed—decided to cancel the concession in November 1932, charging that it was originally obtained by deception. The British government was not about to accept this development, because the loss of Persian petroleum would have constituted a serious blow to the British economy. The British navy made a show of force in the Persian Gulf, and the matter was taken to the League of Nations. As the crisis continued, the British realized that Iran was being forced to seek Soviet help and that the domestic political situation in Iran required a symbolic victory for Riza Shah. Consequently, in April 1933, the APOC signed a new concession with the Persian government that was to be valid until 1993 and that could not be unilaterally revoked by Persia. The new concession provided for a reduction in the area assigned to the APOC, an increase in revenue for Persia, and participation by the Persians in the management of the APOC.[15] However, the Persians came to regard the new concession as producing little benefit for their country. In fact, in later years it was suggested that Riza Shah and the British government deliberately staged the crisis to prolong the British monopoly of Persian petroleum.[16] Whatever the merit of this argument, the enduring perception of the 1933 concession in Iran was that the Persian government had acceded to British demands. And it was this perception that later furnished Musaddiq with the public support to confront the British.

In the aftermath of granting the new concession to the British, Riza Shah was still hoping to bring an American oil company to Iran. It was not until 1936 that the Amiranian Oil Company (a subsidiary of the Seaboard Oil Company of Delaware) secured a concession in northern Iran. The Soviets cooperated by granting Amiranian transportation rights through Russia. But the British once again contended that, on the basis of their claim to the Khoshtaria concession, the petroleum of northern Iran belonged to the Anglo-Iranian Oil Company (AIOC)—the new name for the APOC. The British objection, however, proved to be unnecessary because Amiranian's activities were confined to conducting surveys in northern Iran. The unstable situation in the Soviet Union and the development of oil resources elsewhere convinced the Amiranian Oil Company to give up its concession in 1938.[17] As it turned out, this was to mark Riza Shah's last effort to invite an American oil company to Iran. The outbreak of the Second World War and the subsequent Anglo-Russian invasion of Iran in 1941 sent Riza Shah into exile and made his son, Muhammad Riza, the Shah of Iran. From this point on, and for reasons that were beyond the control of the young Shah, the United States was to display an unprecedented willingness to become involved in Iran.

Among the consequences of World War II were the beginning of the decline of the Anglo-Russian imperial rivalry and the rise of the American-Soviet struggle for power and influence. As documented by archival data, the signs of antagonism between the two emerging superpowers were present in Iran long before the conclusion of the war.[18] The

American policy planners became concerned with Iran, not merely on account of her petroleum, but because of her strategic position as a buffer between the Soviet Union and the important American oil interests on the Arab side of the Persian Gulf. It was this concern, for example, that led to the oil crisis of 1944, when both the United States and the Soviet Union sought concessions in northern Iran, resulting in the decision of the Iranian government to cancel the negotiations altogether.[19] And it was this concern that produced Truman's stand against Stalin in the Azerbaijan crisis of 1946. In brief, though the phrase "Third World countries" was not yet popularized, Iran became a prime example of a country whose destiny was controlled by the pressures of the superpowers' competing strategies—what the Soviets referred to as checking capitalist aggression and what the Americans called containment of Communism.

The monumental changes produced by the Second World War, in conjunction with the history of Persian petroleum, paved the way for the ascendance of Dr. Musaddiq in Iran. Born to a wealthy landlord family in 1880, Muhammad Musaddiq was among the small number of Persians who received a European education. Although Musaddiq was impressed by the democratic institutions of the West, he became convinced that the economic power of Europe, particularly that of Great Britain, was largely based upon the exploitation of weaker states. Then, as a political activist, a member of Parliament, and later as prime minister, Musaddiq adopted the approach that the only way Iran could salvage independence was to deny special privileges to all foreign powers. Musaddiq considered his approach as maintaining a "Negative Equilibrium" among external influences. This was in sharp contrast to the traditional policies of the Persian monarchs, who sought to keep a so-called "Positive Equilibrium" by granting equal privileges to the major powers. What distinguished Musaddiq, however, was not so much the novelty of his method as his ability to evoke the old and yet magical theme of the struggle for national independence.

The political machinery that supported Musaddiq was the National Front, an umbrella party that attracted a mosaic of political figures who shared a feeling of nationalism and a desire to move their crippled society into the twentieth century. The stage was the Iranian Parliament, where Musaddiq and his followers sought to adopt a Western style of open debate and legal procedure to achieve their goals. Starting with the oil crisis of 1944, it was Musaddiq's resolution that produced the law forbidding the Iranian government to negotiate oil concessions without the approval of the Majlis. And in 1947 Musaddiq's followers were responsible for blocking an oil concession promised to the Soviets during the Azerbaijan crisis. More significant, the Majlis asked the Iranian government to look into the AIOC concession of 1933. Such maneuvers, despite their economic ramifications, were all political acts aimed at acquiring some degree of independence.[20]

To deal with an increasingly assertive Majlis, the Shah agreed to renegotiate with the AIOC. The process was slow, and it was not until July of 1949 that the Supplemental Agreement was produced. For all intents and purposes, this was merely a face-lift to the AIOC concession of 1933. As the Shah and a series of his prime ministers were to learn, the Majlis was in no mood to accept such a cosmetic solution. Its final presentation to the Majlis in 1950 by Prime Minister Razmara was greeted with jeers and total rejection. While still on a wild-goose chase after another agreement, Razmara was assassinated in March of 1951, allegedly by a member of a religious group. This act, in conjunction with the attempt on the life of the Shah in 1949, was indicative of the fact that Musaddiq and his followers were moderates compared to the other forces that resented the activities of the AIOC. The Shah began to realize that flirting with the AIOC concession of 1933 was not enough and that Musaddiq and his followers could depend upon widespread public discontent to push for nationalization of the Iranian oil industry.

That the Persians viewed the AIOC as an instrument of British imperialism was in part related to Great Britain's negative image in Iran. At the same time, however, there were specific grievances that aroused hostility toward the AIOC, including: (1) the company's alleged interferences in the domestic politics of Iran; (2) the perception of the company's labor policies as being discriminatory against Iranian nationals; (3) complaints against the high prices for petroleum products charged by the AIOC within Iran; (4) disapproval of the fact that the AIOC paid taxes to the British government but not to Iran; and (5) misgivings concerning the company's method of calculating "profits" that were to be shared with Iran. These misgivings were reinforced by the AIOC's refusal to allow the Iranian government to audit its accounts. In order to show small "profits," the AIOC was allegedly deducting not only every conceivable expense, including generous taxes paid to the British treasury, but also the amount the company invested annually outside Iran. These charges were given credence by the subsequent revelation that by 1950 Iran had received $45 million for her oil, while the AIOC paid $112 million in taxes alone to the British government.[21]

By relying upon the widespread resentment against the AIOC, Musaddiq and the National Front became the catalysts for as well as the guardians of the public demand to nationalize the oil industry. When the idea was first suggested in the Majlis, the British government objected and warned Iran of "the most serious consequences." Despite the British threat, the Majlis turned the idea into law in March of 1951 and recommended to the Shah the appointment of Dr. Musaddiq as prime minister. At this juncture, the Shah had little choice but to accept the whole package and thus hand the government of Iran to Musaddiq. But the British reaction was quite strong. It included the dispatch of an impressive naval force to the Persian Gulf, the total blockade of Iran's transportation facilities, the withdrawal of all British technicians, and a formal complaint to the International Court of Justice. This last measure, though by far the least harmful, particularly incensed Musaddiq, who argued that the court had no jurisdiction to decide whether a sovereign nation had the right to nationalize a given industry within its own borders. Although the International Court initially imposed a restraining order upon the feuding parties, later it accepted Iran's argument and disclaimed jurisdiction.

The effective shutdown of the Iranian oil industry, however, placed Musaddiq in an unenviable position. The already feeble economy of Iran started to crumble, and the political groups that had backed nationalization began wavering in their support. The clergy, led by Mullah Kashani, opposed any conciliatory gesture toward the British, and the Iranian Communists and their Tudeh Party began to emerge as a force with the potential to dominate Iranian politics. Amid this confusion, Musaddiq was hoping to get the British to recognize nationalization, to reach a negotiated settlement, and to allow Iran to export her petroleum. In pursuing such ends, Musaddiq thought he could control domestic politics and gain leverage against the British by relying upon American-Soviet rivalry. As a result, Musaddiq tolerated the Soviets and the activities of the Tudeh Party, while he simultaneously sought economic and military aid from the United States. To break the deadlock in the negotiations with the British, Musaddiq welcomed direct American involvement in the form of mediation by Averell Harriman.

The idea of the Harriman Mission was suggested by Secretary of

State Dean Acheson and was supported by George McGhee, Assistant Secretary of State for Middle Eastern Affairs, and by Paul Nitze, director of the State Department Policy Planning Staff. The British government was not enthusiastic but went along with the idea. President Truman approved the plan, and in a letter to Musaddiq he expressed high hopes for a negotiated settlement. But the odds were stacked against Harriman even before he arrived in Tehran. The news of the Harriman Mission had produced strong reactions in Iran. The expected opposition from the Tudeh Party was merged with objections from Mullah Kashani, who subsequently declared that if Musaddiq acceded to British demands "his blood will flow like Razmara's."[22] There was also disapproval from other National Front members, who contended that American involvement betrayed Musaddiq's policy of "Negative Equilibrium." Finally, adding to Harriman's difficulties was the attitude of Dr. Henry Grady, the American ambassador in Iran, who had ambitions of playing a major role himself and was unhappy about having Harriman in Tehran.[23] Considering this background, the task assigned to Harriman was difficult, if not impossible.

During his stay in Tehran, Harriman—accompanied by Walter Levy and Vernon Walters, who acted as economic advisor and interpreter respectively—had several long conversations with Musaddiq. What immediately became clear to Harriman was that Iran's grievances against the AIOC, while containing economic and political considerations, also reflected Musaddiq's personal vendetta against the British. At their very first meeting, Musaddiq began his anti-British sermon by telling Harriman, "You do not know how crafty they are. You do not know how they sully everything they touch." In response, Harriman explained that the British were like most other people: Some were good, some bad, and most in between. But Musaddiq repeated, "You do not know them. You do not know them." Harriman, somewhat irked, retorted, "Yes, I know them. I was lend-lease expeditor in Great Britain. I have been an Ambassador to Great Britain. We have fought two wars with them which you haven't, and I assure you that they are good and bad and most of all in between." In addition, Harriman and Levy took turns during the long meetings in delivering lectures of their own regarding the "realities" of international oil markets.[24] In the end, however, it appeared that Musaddiq was as impressed by these presentations as Harriman was by Musaddiq's anti-British remarks.

The original British negotiating position indicated that the AIOC wanted to preserve the concession of 1933 in exchange for increasing Iran's share of the profits from about 20 percent to 50 percent. Musaddiq rejected the proposal for two reasons: First, Musaddiq's political constituency was sold on the idea of nationalization; second, as far as Musaddiq was concerned, the increase in the percentage share of the profits was meaningless because Iran had no control over the method by which the profit figure was derived. And if the past behavior of the AIOC was any indication, Musaddiq argued, Iran would be deprived of her share of the oil revenue. Consequently, the British proposed a new formula, which became the basis of Harriman's mediation efforts.

According to this formula, the British were prepared to accept nationalization if Iran paid compensation to the AIOC and if a British technical company with a British general manager was put in charge of oil production. Although Musaddiq argued against compensation—on the grounds that the AIOC was more than compensated by its huge profits—he was willing to accept a settlement. But in view of the anti-British sentiment in Iran, the idea of giving the British authority over oil production was politically unacceptable. The ensuing conflict over who should be in charge of oil production, and the publicity given to the issue in the Iranian media, poisoned Harriman's efforts to produce a negotiated settlement. Subsequently, the British were depicted as being solely responsible for the failure of the negotiations—a verdict that was not only advertised in Iran but that was also expressed by American press correspondents still sympathetic to Musaddiq.[25]

Contrary to this perception, however, Great Britain's desire to have control over the oil production was not totally unjustified. If the AIOC was to be compensated with Iranian oil, then the successful operation of the oil industry was the first prerequisite. Iran's lack of technicians to operate the oil industry, and the fact that other Western oil companies, including the Americans, were unprepared to become involved, had added to the British concern. As explained by Anthony Eden, the foreign secretary of Churchill's government, "In this instance compensation could, in effect, only be paid in the form of oil, therefore the industry had to be restarted with efficient management and an assured future."[26]

Although still thinking of encouraging a negotiated settlement, the American policy planners were becoming increasingly concerned with the consequences of Musaddiq's confrontation with the British. In the words of Paul Nitze:

We in the Policy Planning Staff were sensitive to the impact of the international oil business on the U.K. balance of payments and on the stability of the pound. We were concerned by the growing influence of the Tudeh Party, which was a Moscow-oriented Communist Party, and the danger that economic collapse would bring the Soviet controlled world down to the Persian Gulf. Further, we were concerned that oil, in the control of unfriendly hands, could be used against the West.[27]

Against this background, Musaddiq came to the United States in October of 1951 to appear before the UN Security Council and to respond to charges brought against Iran by Great Britain. After delivering an emotional speech before the UN, a tired and ailing Musaddiq went to Washington and was taken to Walter Reed Hospital by George McGhee and Paul Nitze. In subsequent weeks, the two American officials had a series of discussions with Musaddiq in which McGhee played the role of the "great and good friend of Iran" and Paul Nitze the "villain" who insisted upon those things not attractive to Musaddiq. At one point, Musaddiq sarcastically asked Mr. Nitze whether his real name was Levy, referring to Walter Levy, whom Musaddiq had grown to dislike during the Harriman Mission.[28]

When Musaddiq visited the White House in late 1951, he sought to gain American sympathy by describing Iran as a very poor country covered with desert sand. President Truman did not challenge his guest, but Acheson, clearly running out of patience, snapped back, "and with your oil, rather like Texas!" Acheson did not think that Musaddiq was a Communist. But considering what Acheson did think of him, Musaddiq's image could not have suffered much more even if he had been a Communist. As revealed by the following statement, Acheson loathed not only Musaddiq's policies but also his appearance:

> He [Musaddiq] reminded me very strongly of a character in a play of Barrie's—Dear Brutus—blob. He was completely bald; he had no hair on his head at all, and a long, beak-like face which came out of his long nose.... He had a funny, bird-like quality; he made quick little movements like a bird jumping about on a perch. I think he must have been an extraordinary gambler. He took the most terrible chances; he daily ran into a frenzy.... And there's no doubt, I think, that he sowed the wind and reaped the whirlwind.[29]

Acheson's British counterpart and look-alike, Anthony Eden, who was in Washington at the time, also perceived Musaddiq as "the first

Secretary of State Dean Acheson talking with Iranian Premier Muhammad Musaddiq at Walter Reed Hospital. Washington, D.C., November 13, 1951. (Source: Harris & Ewing)

real bit of meat to come the way of the cartoonists since the war."[30] Eden had come to Washington with new proposals that called for the participation of American oil companies in marketing Persian petroleum. It was hoped that this plan would reduce Musaddiq's anxiety concerning British involvement in oil production. More significant, it was intended to present Musaddiq with a joint Anglo-American position. As Eden remembered, so complete was the Anglo-American understanding that "it was agreed that there was no object in encouraging Musaddiq to stay longer in Washington."[31] And in order to present Musaddiq with a *fait accompli,* it was decided to push the new plan after Musaddiq's departure from the United States. Subsequently, Loy Henderson was appointed as the new American ambassador to Iran and was given the task of presenting Musaddiq with the new formula. In the early months of 1952, Henderson tried to get Musaddiq to accept the joint Anglo-American approach. But Musaddiq saw the new proposal as another cunning scheme by the British and refused to accept it.

To make matters worse, whatever had remained of government stability in Iran began to wither away. Although the National Front had managed to produce a solid victory in the election of January 1952, Musaddiq was losing control. Anti-British protests were rampant in Iran, and the Tudeh members used the opportunity to stage anti-American demonstrations. To cope with Iran's internal crisis, Musaddiq sought to increase his power in July 1952 by demanding control over the armed forces. At this juncture, the Shah refused to give away the last symbol of his power and exercised his constitutional right to dismiss Musaddiq. The Shah then appointed Qavam—the old politician who had handled the Azerbaijan crisis—to the post of prime minister. But violent pro-Musaddiq demonstrations immediately forced the Shah to reinstate Musaddiq and to watch helplessly as Musaddiq claimed control over the army. Nevertheless, the army as a whole remained uncommitted to Musaddiq, a factor that was to facilitate his overthrow in the following year.

There is no doubt that by the end of 1952 Musaddiq's government had very little credibility in the United States. The process had begun early in the year when the perceptions of American officials were transmitted to the American media, which then took it upon itself to publicly ridicule Musaddiq. A most condescending attitude, for example, was displayed by *Time* Magazine's lurid portrait of Musaddiq as the Man of the Year in January 1952.[32] Then came criticism of Musaddiq because of two more lost opportunities—one at the beginning of 1952 and the other in August of that year—to reach an agreement with the British. Musaddiq's continuous efforts to push aside the Shah, the complete breakdown of diplomatic relations with Great Britain, and the growing power of the Tudeh Party in Iran added the finishing touches to his negative image in the United States. As described by Acheson, Musaddiq came to be viewed as a tragic figure who sowed the wind and reaped the whirlwind.

But the uncertainty as to what would follow if Musaddiq's government should crumble, and the possibility of a Communist takeover in Iran, persuaded the lame-duck Truman administration to launch a last-ditch effort toward a negotiated settlement at the end of 1952.[33] To get British approval, Paul Nitze made two trips to Britain and consulted with Anthony Eden. According to this final package, the question of compensation for the AIOC was to be settled by an arbitration panel, with the British dropping the oil blockade and the United

States extending $50 million to Iran in exchange for future delivery of petroleum. The British involvement in Iran was also to be reduced by the participation of American oil companies. Apparently, Musaddiq was willing to accept this plan even though he lacked domestic support for such a move. When Eisenhower was elected president, however, Musaddiq backed away from the agreement. This was interpreted in Washington as another scheme by Musaddiq to get a better deal from the new administration.[34]

THE SOLUTION EISENHOWER ACCEPTED

Just before Eisenhower's inauguration in January 1953, Musaddiq wrote to the President-elect complaining about the British and asking for American understanding and sympathy. While referring to American support for the British, Musaddiq wondered whether the United States "which has such an exalted moral standing in the world can afford to support the internationally immoral policy of a friend and ally merely in order not to disturb good relations with that friend and ally." In responding to Musaddiq, Eisenhower wrote, "I hope you accept my assurances that I have in no way compromised our position of impartiality in this matter and that no individual has attempted to prejudice me in the matter. This leads me to observe that I hope our own future relationship will be completely free of any suspicion, but on the contrary will be characterized by confidence and trust inspired by frankness and friendliness."[35]

Despite Eisenhower's upbeat reply, however, Musaddiq had already become expendable. A representative of the oil industry had already informed Eisenhower in November of 1952 that Musaddiq was the source of a "prairie fire" that could consume American strategic interests.[36] John Foster Dulles had already expressed the conviction that Musaddiq was a hopeless person and that it was "inherently wrong to pursue a negotiated settlement unless the political picture in Iran was changed."[37] American military planners had already been involved in discussions concerning the possibility of direct military action in Iran.[38] CIA Director Bedell Smith and Deputy Director Allen Dulles had already been approached by the British with a plan to overthrow Musaddiq. And Kermit Roosevelt had already been to London in

November of 1952 to discuss the covert operation. In fact, Bedell Smith was so anxious that he had summoned Kermit Roosevelt to his office and had wanted to know, "When are those blanking British coming to talk to us? And when is our goddam operation going to get underway?" To which Kermit Roosevelt replied, "As soon after Inauguration Day as you and JFD can see them."[39]

Early in February 1953 the British contingent showed up in Washington. At a meeting with American officials, including John Foster Dulles, Allen Dulles, Bedell Smith, and Kermit Roosevelt, the subject of the covert operation was discussed in detail. The British proposed making Kermit Roosevelt the field commander of the operation. There was some hesitation on the part of American officials. Finally, from behind a cloud of pipe smoke came the voice of John Foster Dulles saying "Yes." Then it was decided that the man who should replace Musaddiq as prime minister was Fazlullah Zahidi, an Iranian general who had been suspected of pro-Nazi activities during World War II. Kermit Roosevelt assured everyone in the room that Zahidi was anti-Soviet and that he did not "retain any Anti-British sentiments." The British seemed unsure of this selection but went along. In the end, John Foster Dulles pushed back his chair and lumbered to his feet. "I guess that's about all we can do now," he said gruffly. "Meeting adjourned!"[40]

Winston Churchill and Anthony Eden had already approved the plan to overthrow Musaddiq. And there were no doubts in the minds of American officials that Eisenhower would concur.[41] They were all aware of Eisenhower's belief that the security and economic well-being of the United States' European friends, particularly the British, were indispensable to American strategic interests. The Anglo-American consensus was also a direct result of major developments that had taken place in the Middle East by the end of 1952. England and France, which had dominated that region in the past, were no longer able to exercise their authority. The emergence of an independent Israel and its subsequent conflicts with Arab states had led to greater tension in the area. Nasser and friends had managed to overthrow the Egyptian monarchy and had become involved in a bitter dispute with the British over the Suez Canal. The fate of Afghanistan had become a source of concern because the Soviets had been pressing that country for exploration rights to petroleum.[42] In conjunction with the turmoil in Iran, there had been disturbances in Iraq and Lebanon, which had prompted British diplomats to conclude that such events were "contagious" and were spread by Communist agents.[43] Finally, a CIA estimate in December 1952 had predicted that "the Kremlin will probably conduct an increasingly active political warfare campaign in the Middle East and Africa ... the Communists will probably concentrate upon efforts to establish common fronts with the nationalists and other anti-Western groups."[44]

The American concern with the Middle East and Iran was given expression in the meeting of the National Security Council in January 1953. "The United States should make its interests in the area of the Middle East and South Asia more explicit," stated the NSC. "It should be recognized that diminished British power will require the United States to assume an increasing responsibility in the area. ... "[45] What this essentially meant was that the United States had accepted the responsibility of finding quick solutions to problems that had been created by long years of European colonial policies. As later became evident, American policy postulated that, if Western interests and Third World nationalism could not be reconciled, then the latter had to be subdued and controlled. Therefore, Musaddiq became a prime target, not merely because of his activities in Iran, but also because of the effects of his policies in the Third World. Although it seemed that Eisenhower was genuinely concerned about the possibility of a Communist takeover in Iran, the fact remained that a neutral and otherwise independent Musaddiq still could not fit into the Churchill-Eden-Eisenhower-Dulles perception of world affairs. Whereas Eisenhower and Dulles were mindful of the loss of Western influence in the Middle East, Churchill and Eden were actually insulted that the likes of Nasser of Egypt and Musaddiq of Iran had the audacity to challenge British domination.

"Winston is trying to relive the days of World War II," Eisenhower recorded on January 6, 1953. "In those days he had the enjoyable feeling that he and our President were sitting on some rather Olympian platform with respect to the rest of the world and directing world affairs from that point of vantage." Eisenhower gathered this impression during a conversation with Churchill in New York that included a discussion of Anglo-American policies toward Musaddiq. "Winston does not by any means propose to resort to power politics and to disregard legitimate aspirations among weaker peoples," Eisenhower continued. "But he does take the rather old-fashioned, paternalistic approach that since we, with our experience and power, will be required to support and carry the heavy burdens of decent international plans, as well as aid infant nations towards self-dependence, other nations should recognize the wisdom of our suggestions and follow them." Then Eisenhower offered his own conclusions: "This is true—in abstract. But we can not expect that it will be accepted unless we convince others by persuasion and example. Long and patient negotiations, understanding, and equality of treatment will have to be used."[46]

Eisenhower's departure from a relatively liberal stand and his acceptance of Churchill's strategy were conditioned by the importance attached to the control of Iran. As early as April 1951, Eisenhower had written in his diary, "Lord knows what we would do without the Iranian oil."[47] Eisenhower's anxiety was further increased by subsequent events in Iran. As a result, Eisenhower moved from sympathy with the British view during Churchill's visit in January 1953 to total agreement with the British by the time Eden came to the United States in March of that year. Eden found the American president "obsessed" with the problem of Iran and prepared to follow through with the plan to replace Musaddiq. According to Eden, Eisenhower expressed concern that "the consequences of an extension of Russian control of Iran, which he regarded as a distinct possibility, would either involve the loss of the Middle East oil supplies or the threat of another world war."[48]

Among the reasons for Eisenhower's outlook was the uncertainty created by the death of Stalin in the first week of March. In examining its consequences, the CIA had introduced the following note of caution: "The death of Stalin removed an autocrat who, while ruthless and determined to spread Soviet power, did not allow his ambitions to lead him into reckless courses of action in his foreign policy. It would be unsafe to assume that the new Soviet regime will have Stalin's skill in avoiding war."[49] This assessment went a long way toward convincing the Eisenhower administration that, if the Communists were to take over in Iran, the possibility of direct American military action might pose a much greater risk than previously anticipated. Therefore, the desirability of a speedy covert operation began to appear greater than ever before.

Meanwhile, Musaddiq continued to sow the wind. In May 1953, he wrote another letter to Eisenhower complaining about the British. In asking for increased American assistance, Musaddiq lamented that thus far it had not been "sufficient to solve the problems of Iran and to ensure world peace which is the aim and ideal of the noble people and of the Government of the United States." Eisenhower took more than a month to reply, and when he did, he coldly rebuffed Musaddiq. In the absence of an oil agreement, the President said, many American citizens would be opposed to assistance to Iran. Then Eisenhower offered a warning that proved to be prophetic. "I note the concern reflected in your letter at the present dangerous situation in Iran," Eisenhower stated, "and sincerely hope that before it is too late, the Government of Iran will take such steps as are in its power to prevent a further deterioration of that situation."[50]

Musaddiq ignored this warning primarily because he did not have the domestic support necessary for a negotiated settlement—at least not for the kind of settlement that the British had been demanding. Moreover, the social unrest in Iran had already assumed a life of its own, going beyond the oil dispute and beyond Musaddiq's control. The rising power of the Tudeh Party and the disintegration of Musaddiq's support within the National Front had placed the Iranian government in a precarious position. To widen his political support, Musaddiq had appointed Tudeh members to his cabinet. But the action had further divided the National Front, and the ensuing conflicts compelled Musaddiq to dissolve the Majlis in July 1953. In the meantime, the Tudeh members had been calling for the removal of the Shah and had been attacking Musaddiq for his failure to publicly denounce the institution of monarchy. And to top it all, the Soviets had dispatched Anatol Laurentiev—the man who had masterminded the Communist takeover of Czechoslovakia in 1948—as the new Soviet ambassador to Iran. Whereas the significance of such developments might have escaped the beleaguered Musaddiq, it served notice to Washington that further delay in an American response would lead to most serious and perhaps irreversible consequences.

That the American response came in the form of "Operation Ajax" had a great deal to do with the widening gap between American interests and power. As detailed in Chapter 5, by the time Eisenhower had assumed office, the active extension of containment throughout the Third World had become the most troublesome aspect of balancing American power with expanded commitments. American involvement in the Korean conflict had taken its toll, leaving Eisenhower with the task of ending the war without eroding American prestige. More significant, the Korean conflict had shown with absolute clarity the undesirability of limited war. In brief, the rising cost of containment by conventional means, the development of covert capabilities, and the uncertainty as to how the Soviets would react in the immediate post-Stalin era made "Operation Ajax" appear to be the most sensible course of action.

Despite the decision to carry out the covert operation, however, the possibility of direct military action by the United States was never ruled out. Although some of the relevant information has since been released by the JCS and the NSC, the subject has received little attention in scholarly analyses. This may be related in part to the confusing format and language of most JCS and NSC documents and to the inconsistency with which such documents were later declassified.[51] Nevertheless, some clues to American military strategy with regard to Musaddiq's Iran can be extracted from recently declassified documents.

An early reference to American military strategy in Iran appeared in a JCS memorandum of October 1952, which stated that the JCS was considering "feasible U.S. military course of action." Then a series of specific proposals was introduced in January 1953 and was subsequently developed by the JCS. The initial proposal for possible military action called for: "a) Air shows of force over Iran. b) Additional arms aid to appropriate Middle East countries. c) Deployment of U.S. Air Force units to Southern Turkey. d) Deployment of U.S. forces to the vicinity of Basra, Iraq."[52]

According to the JCS documents, the NSC had requested military options, and repeated references were made to NSC 107/2 and NSC 136/1.[53] The stated purpose of the initial plan was to deploy American forces "in the event of a Tudeh coup in Iran." But by the summer of 1953, the chairman of the JCS, Admiral Radford, was told by the NSC to prepare for emergency action "since the United States might be requested by the Shah of Iran to provide some degree of military support." As a result, a revised version of possible military action was put forward at the same time that the covert operation was underway. This emergency plan specified the following American strategy: "a) Deploy ground and air forces to Tehran and other major cities to restore order. b) Deploy ground and air forces to Abadan to protect the oil installations. c) Deploy a carrier task group to the Persian Gulf to support friendly forces in southern Iran."[54]

In light of the available information, it appears that if the covert operation were to fail the United States was contemplating military intervention in Iran. Considering the danger of Soviet reaction, and considering the absence of domestic consensus in the United States for another conventional war, the very fact that American policy planners were even considering military action was indicative of the importance attached to the control of Iran. As it turned out, however, there was no need for the emergency military plan. Kermit Roosevelt took one million dollars to Tehran, spent about one hundred thousand dollars, and, with help from his Iranian friends, got everything fixed up just as Churchill and Eisenhower wanted.

The main features of "Operation Ajax" consisted of paying a group of Tehran hoodlums to create street demonstrations and to incite the general public against Musaddiq. As might be expected, the key to the operation was getting the support of the army officers, whose rank and file had little loyalty toward Musaddiq. According to plan, the Shah dismissed Musaddiq and appointed General Zahidi as the new prime minister. At first, Musaddiq refused to bow out, and with the aid of a few army friends, he arrested the Shah's messenger. The Shah then flew out of Iran and ended up in Rome, where he conferred with CIA Director Allen Dulles. But a few days later, the hired mob hit the streets shouting pro-Shah slogans and clashing with Musaddiq supporters and Tudeh members. The army officers who were cooperating with Roosevelt provided support for the pro-Shah demonstrations. As the mob rampaged through the streets of Tehran, it was joined by many soldiers in civilian clothing; the throng headed for Musaddiq's residence. Musaddiq was able to escape but shortly thereafter was arrested and put in jail. The celebration began in the American Embassy in Tehran, with caviar and whisky boosting the high spirits of the participants. The Shah returned to Iran triumphantly, with a crowd of well-wishers greeting him, while most Iranians remained confused about how quickly everything had changed.

During the implementation of "Operation Ajax," several hundred Iranians were killed and scores of others were injured.[55] But everything considered, it was a smooth operation, producing fewer casualties than a direct military action would have done. Musaddiq was given a mock trial, kept in prison for three years, and then put under house arrest, where he later died quietly. Musaddiq's top aides as well as many Tudeh members were either executed, imprisoned, or forced into exile. This was the beginning of a "house cleaning" by the Shah that in later years became so pervasive as to endanger the life of any Iranian citizen who dared to question the wisdom of his policies.

When the mission was completed, Kermit Roosevelt left Tehran, leaving the remaining CIA money (about $900,000) with his Iranian friends until further aid from the United States could arrive. On the way home, he stopped in London and paid a visit to Churchill. "We met at your Cousin Franklin's, did we not?" Churchill asked. "I thought so. Well you have an exciting story to tell. I am anxious to hear it." Kermit Roosevelt recited the dramatic highlights of the covert operation. "Young man," Churchill exclaimed at the end of the two-hour visit, "if I had been but a few years younger, I would have loved nothing better than to have served under your command in this great venture!"[56]

Churchill had good reason to be cheerful. Musaddiq was in prison, and the Iranian oil industry was being carved up in a manner that benefited the British the most. The so-called settlement of the oil dispute finally came down to the following arrangement. Iran was allowed to keep an apparatus by the name of the National Iranian Oil Company (NIOC). Then it was decided that the NIOC would surrender all rights to the production and marketing of petroleum through a concession to a consortium of international oil companies. In exchange, Iran was to receive 50 percent of the profits that the consortium was willing to acknowledge through its bookkeeping. Under this plan, the British-owned AIOC—later called British Petroleum (BP)—became the consortium's single largest shareholder, with 40 percent of the shares. Another 40 percent was divided equally among American oil companies—Gulf Oil, Socony-Vacuum (Mobil), Standard Oil of New Jersey, and Texaco. The remaining 20 percent was divided between Royal Dutch (14 percent) and Compagnie Francaise de Petroles (6 percent).

The British AIOC actually received more than 40 percent if its interest in Royal Dutch was taken into account. To put the icing on the cake, Iran was required to pay £25,000,000 as compensation to the AIOC for canceling its concession of 1933 and for allowing the new consortium to begin operation. In addition, the AIOC was to receive $600,000,000 in compensation from the new consortium. Of course, this cost to the consortium was then figured into its profit calculations, which further reduced the amount to be paid to the Iranian government.[57] What made such an arrangement possible was the fact that the Shah was both grateful to and fearful of those who had put him back in power. As a result, the Shah not only accepted the whole package but worked diligently to adorn the agreement with legal trimmings. The politically castrated Majlis was made to ratify the agreement in October

British Prime Minister Winston Churchill gives President Eisenhower a final handshake just before leaving the White House at the end of their weekend conference on international problems. June 29, 1954. (Source: Associated Press)

1954. The vote was 113 to 5 with one abstention and with nine deputies absent.

The new oil agreement was hailed in London and in Washington as a "milestone" in constructive friendship between Great Britain and the United States. John Foster Dulles declared that the oil settlement was an "entirely equitable arrangement" and offered his congratulations to Premier Zahidi, who had been selected by the CIA to replace Musaddiq. The Shah was congratulated by Eisenhower and was told, "You personally have made a valuable contribution." President Eisenhower also expressed affection for Iran and admiration for the Shah's overall leadership. "Like myself," Eisenhower stated, "all Americans have a deep concern for the well-being of Iran. With them I have watched closely your courageous efforts, your steadfastness over the past difficult years, and with them I have hoped that you might achieve the goals you so earnestly desire. The attainment of an oil settlement along the lines which have been announced should be a significant step in the direction of the realization of your aspirations for your people."

In responding to Eisenhower, the Shah was most cordial, but he could not bring himself to completely ignore his own predicament. "I can not sufficiently lay stress on the fact that American assistance to Iran has been most timely and helpful," the Shah wrote to Eisenhower. "My people reciprocate to the full the friendship of your noble nation." But in referring to the oil settlement, the Shah stated, "in light of present world conditions, [it] appears to be as equitable a solution of a difficult problem as could have been reached."[58] Undoubtedly, the most relevant of "world conditions" to the Shah was his personal predicament in being reinstated by the CIA. The fate of Musaddiq was a constant reminder to the Shah of the fragility of his own position, a factor that not only shaped his dealings with the West but also became the precursor of the oppressive policies that he imposed upon his people in later years.

PERSPECTIVE

In simplest terms, Musaddiq may be described as a Third World nationalist who fought but failed to overcome British imperial policies in Iran. Yet such a description, though it contains a core of truth, still leaves out more than it includes. Although Musaddiq's message resembled those uttered by other Third World nationalists, there was an uncommon seriousness in his challenge. Part of what separated Musaddiq from most Third World crusaders was that he was not struggling for a mere symbolic victory, such as declaring a cosmetic independence, flying a new flag, and playing a new national anthem. Musaddiq's attempt to end the British monopoly of Persian petroleum was as serious a challenge as ever posed by a Third World leader. And, of course, the nature of Musaddiq's challenge had a great deal to do with his final predicament. Whereas Churchill and Eisenhower were willing to tolerate symbolic victories by the Third World, they were not inclined to allow the control of vital resources like petroleum to slip away.

Among the factors contributing to Musaddiq's misfortune were his misconceptions of the West. Despite being educated in the West, or perhaps because of it, Musaddiq had acquired a somewhat romantic and unrealistic view of Western political culture. As revealed by his later actions, Musaddiq tended to separate the imperialism of Western governments from the will of their general public. Consequently, when Musaddiq won his case before the International Court of Justice, he was expecting sympathy and support from the people of the West. And when Musaddiq visited the United States in 1951, he presented the plight of his country before the UN, once again expecting public opinion in the West to come to his rescue. In harboring these expectations, Musaddiq was conditioned by his belief that the so-called common folks in Western societies cared enough about global justice to compel their governments to act accordingly.

But as noted in Chapter 1, Musaddiq's expectations reflected his failure to come to grips with the reality that the behavior of Western democracies is, at bottom, a reflection of the attitude of their collectivities; that the weight assigned to the concepts of liberty and justice within nations has little bearing upon their international conduct, especially when it concerns competition over vital resources; that the general public in the West, very much like their counterparts the world over, is concerned with their own self-interest and is otherwise unwilling to endanger their privileges in the name of global justice; and that the imperialism of powerful states is made possible not because of the conspiracy of their elite but because of the consensus of the society below.

Musaddiq's repeated efforts to invite American involvement in Iran also went beyond the game of realpolitik and reflected his belief that the United States—a nation that had granted her own citizens an unprecedented degree of liberty—would seek to free the subjugated nations from the yoke of European imperialism. Because of the nobility of American ideals, and because of a desperate need for hope, Musaddiq came to view the United States as a savior. As a result, America was placed upon a pedestal and was expected to behave unlike all other empires of the past. In adopting such exalted expectations, Musaddiq lost sight of the fact that economic and military considerations had imposed narrow limits upon the extent to which any nation could be expected to transcend its own immediate self-interest.

Finally, Musaddiq's failure to understand the special nature of Anglo-American relations made him appear—in Acheson's words—as a tragic figure who sowed the wind and reaped the whirlwind. Musaddiq's poor judgment was demonstrated by his decision to bad-mouth the British before, of all people, Averell Harriman. Even more pathetic was

Musaddiq's effort to seek Eisenhower's help against Churchill. Apparently, Musaddiq was ignorant of the fact that Eisenhower thought so highly of Churchill that he would actually paint a portrait of him. In a broader sense, Musaddiq failed to appreciate the significance of both Anglo-American cultural affinities and the common interests that linked the foreign policies of the United States and Great Britain. As a rule, history had not been kind to those who committed such blunders, and Musaddiq was no exception.

Apart from his mishandling of Iran's foreign policy, Musaddiq's method of dealing with domestic politics went a long way toward bringing about his demise. Like most Third World nationalists, Musaddiq attempted to capture the attention of his countrymen by glorifying their distant past, by disclaiming their recent past, and by blaming their present malaise upon foreign powers. In doing so, Musaddiq sought to reduce the despair of his people and to give them hope that, in the absence of foreign interference, they were capable of achieving great goals. But despite Musaddiq's good intentions, his message often created more problems than it solved. In the case of Iran in the early 1950s, it meant developing false expectations that the country had the technological ability to operate its own oil industry. Therefore, when the British technicians were pulled out of Iran, it led to widespread public discontent because of the inability of Musaddiq's government to run the Iranian oil industry.

The decision of the Eisenhower administration to overthrow Musaddiq was reinforced by Musaddiq's inability to control the emotions that he had helped to unleash in Iran. The public discontent in Iran, which at first fueled Musaddiq's crusade, turned out to be his worst enemy as the original goal of opposing British imperialism became subordinated to the internal struggle for power. By the arrival of 1953, Iran resembled an old ship swept away by a storm with no one aboard capable of dealing with the attendant frenzy. And by the time "Operation Ajax" was implemented, Musaddiq was barely holding on to the broken sails of his sinking ship. Everything considered, whatever might be said of the morality or the legality of American action, it still should not be characterized as having overthrown a stable regime in Iran.

From the vantage point of the Eisenhower administration, replacing Musaddiq was in the interests of the United States, Great Britain, and Iran. Undoubtedly, the politics of petroleum and Iran's place in American-Soviet rivalry played the major roles in Eisenhower's decision. But

Eisenhower was also convinced that he was helping Iran. Similarly, the man who was in charge of the covert operation seemed equally convinced of the nobility of his mission. During interviews with this writer, Kermit Roosevelt explained his involvement in terms of patriotism for his country and a firm conviction that he was also saving Iran from Communism. "Perhaps we could be blamed for misjudging the future development of the Shah," Mr. Roosevelt offered, "but you must remember that in 1953 Musaddiq was handing Iran to the Communists and the Shah appeared to be an idealistic young man who wanted to help his people."[59]

Despite the good intentions of American officials, the consequences of their action left a negative influence in Iran. In examining this influence, however, it is imperative to distinguish between the consequences of Eisenhower's decision and the factors that in later years poisoned American-Iranian relations. To suggest that the overthrow of Musaddiq in itself sowed the seeds of future trouble is to misread history. It should be noted that the people of Iran, with the exception of a very small group, were unaware of American involvement in the overthrow of Musaddiq. It was not until years later that fragmented information began to surface, and even then it remained confined to gossip among the urban population of Iran. Finally, it was not until the onset of the Revolution of 1979 that the majority of Iranians became fully informed of American involvement in the events of 1953. In brief, dissatisfaction with the Shah's policies preceded by many years the public knowledge that he was reinstated in power by the United States.

Similarly, it appears overly optimistic to assume that if Musaddiq had remained in power the chances of democracy in Iran would have been enhanced. The possibility of a Communist takeover notwithstanding, Musaddiq's actions, such as dissolving the Majlis and attempting to control the army, did not bode well for the sharing of power or the establishment of a constitutional government. Furthermore, if the fate of countries similar to Iran was any indication, the odds were against Musaddiq's ability to bring democracy to Iran. For example, the fact that Nasser was permitted to remain in power did very little to introduce democracy to Egypt. In the final analysis, to blame the Eisenhower administration for aborting democratic processes in Iran is not only inaccurate but tends to obscure the true nature of Eisenhower's responsibility in damaging long-term American interests in Iran.

The extent to which the Eisenhower administration was responsible for fostering anti-American sentiments in Iran did not lie so much in the overthrow of Musaddiq as in the decision to allow the British and the American oil companies to take over the Iranian oil industry. Unlike the Anglo-American participation in the overthrow of Musaddiq, the Anglo-American partnership in carving up the Iranian oil industry could not be concealed. As a result, for the first time in the history of American-Iranian relations, the people of Iran began to associate the United States with British imperial policies. Moreover, the Persians felt betrayed in their own exalted expectations of the United States. Consequently, the savior image that the United States had enjoyed in Iran began to crumble, paving the way toward a more critical and unflattering perception of the American role in Iran. From that point on, the ever-increasing American involvement in Iran reflected a special understanding with the Shah's government rather than the wishes of the Iranian people. In brief, the imposition of the oil agreement of 1954 marked the beginning of the "post-invitation" period in American involvement in Iran.

Epilogue: A Critical Appraisal of American Strategies

At least as far back as Woodrow Wilson, American leaders had chosen to mix morality with foreign policy and to encourage exalted expectations of their ability to redress global injustice. The morality play continued in the post–World War II era as the United States became the self-proclaimed savior of Third World countries combating internal problems and the external threat of Communism. America also became the self-proclaimed promoter of the cause of liberal democracy abroad. In projecting this image, the American leaders left themselves open to charges of hypocrisy and managed to confuse some of their own people as well as that portion of the outside world in search of a savior.

The confusion arose because America's morality play did not prevent her from behaving, in various areas of the world and at various times, like an imperialist power. But Americans seemed both embarrassed about admitting their imperialism and unprepared in accepting its responsibilities. Consequently, save for America's success in controlling a handful of small states, the general picture of American imperialism in the Third World has been spasmodic, incoherent, and often counterproductive. What has militated against American interests, however, has not been imperialism per se but poor management of imperialism.

American involvement in Iran reveals many features of this general pattern. The Persian authorities as well as the people of Iran seemed enthusiastic about inviting American influence in their country. With the emergence of American-Soviet rivalry, and because of Iran's strategic significance, the American policymakers were quite willing to accept the invitation and to assign top priority to the control of Iran. Franklin D. Roosevelt began the process by giving special attention to the territorial integrity of Iran during the Tehran Conference. President Truman, by his own admission, was prepared to go to war in 1946 to prevent Stalin from controlling Iran. In 1953 President Eisenhower spoke of the possibility of World War III if the Soviets attempted to dominate Iran. Their successors, each offering various security guarantees, sought to keep Iran within the American sphere of influence. Yet, despite accepting high risks to check Soviet advances, the American leaders generally ignored the internal problems of Iran, which in later years proved damaging to the United States' interests.

From chanting "Long live America" in 1946, the political activists in Iran went to shouting "Death to America" in 1979. This dramatic change in perception, though indicative of the ageless and fundamental political divisions of Iran, still had much to tell about the triumphs and tragedies of American involvement in that country. Admittedly, the historical setting that witnessed the eruption of the simmering rage in Iran was fostered by the internal political dynamics of that country—an ancient land awakened by the power of petroleum, stunned by the rapid infusion of Western influence, and suffocated by a mediocre dictator. Nevertheless, there was an unmistakable American connection. The long-standing American support of the Shah, and the presence of more than sixty thousand Americans in Iran by the mid-1970s, had firmly associated the United States with the policies of the Shah. It was this association that nurtured the roots of the monstrous drama later faced by President Carter.

There is no denying that the Shah was a loyal friend to the United States. Some years after his death, American leaders still mention his name with gratitude. The latest manifestation of this came during the campaign debates in 1984, when President Reagan referred to the Shah as a valuable ally and volunteered his opinion that "he carried the load for us in that part of the world." Of course, President Reagan's statement was in line with what American leaders had been saying since World War II. The principal question, therefore, is not whether the United States should have supported the Shah, but what the nature of that support should have been. In other words, what is being disputed here is not the logic of American policy in befriending the ruler of a client state, but the efficacy of American strategies in protecting that client state and preventing it from falling into the hands of America's enemies.

Before any evaluation can be made of American policies in Iran, however, two basic questions must be addressed: (1) Did the United States have enough leverage to guide the Shah's policies? (2) What advice or program of action might have saved the Shah from his final humiliation? Answers to these questions may yield a yardstick by which the efficacy of American strategies can be measured. In examining the first question, consider the following. During World War II and in the immediate postwar period—when the Iranian treasury was bankrupt—the Shah depended heavily upon the United States for financial and military assistance, not to mention for his personal whims, such as his plea for a small airplane to fly him to his various palaces. In 1946 his country, and in 1953 his throne, were saved by American intervention. In the ensuing years, particularly the era marking the rise in oil revenue, the United States became both the chief buyer of Iran's petroleum and the principal supplier of military hardware. The Shah's massive armed forces—300,000 army, 81,000 air force, and 18,500 navy—were conceived by consulting American military planners, trained by American soldiers, and supervised by American military advisors. And to top it all, much of the Shah's personal fortune, as well as Iran's foreign exchange reserves, was stashed away in American banks.

To say that the Shah was susceptible to counsel from Washington is an understatement. Despite developing an overblown ego, the Shah was desperately dependent upon the United States, a fact well known to the Shah's officials and to the long line of American ambassadors to Iran. Some American diplomats, such as John Wiley—ambassador to Iran during 1948–50—viewed the Shah as something of a cartoon character and often dispatched reports to Washington that rivaled the best pages of comic books. Other American representatives may have taken the Shah more seriously, but they all knew that the Shah was their man in the Middle East. Apparently, the Shah was so accustomed to receiving instruction from Washington that even at the hour of gravest danger he remained hesitant to make a move without first asking for American approval. According to an account published in the *Washington Post*'s issue of January 13, 1980, Ambassador William Sullivan and General Robert Huyser—the two American officials who guided the Shah through the Iranian revolution—conceded that the Shah had no initiative of his own and was simply waiting for orders from Washington.

By quoting authoritative sources in the State Department, National Security Council, and Pentagon, the *Washington Post* article disclosed that "the Shah's departure was being discussed as a serious option by early 1977" and that, once the Shah's downfall became imminent, General Huyser, second in command of all U.S. forces in Europe, went to Iran in the first days of January 1979 "to pull the rug out on the Shah." General Huyser's marching orders, as described by the *Post*'s article, included:

> 1. To tell the shah that his days were numbered: a new day was dawning in Iran, the U.S. policy of support had changed, and he was "to see it our way" or economic pressure would be applied "until he saw it our way."
>
> 2. To tell the shah that he was to leave Iran immediately, since his presence was a continuing source of unrest among the country's top military leaders.
>
> 3. To stop any pro-shah military coup and clear the way for Khomeni's return by warning the U.S.-trained generals that if they moved to seize power the United States would cut off all aid.

The *Washington Post*'s story certainly lends credence to the speculation that, having viewed the Shah's position as hopeless, the United States government sought to speed up his downfall with the intention of avoiding a bloody civil war in Iran. The Shah himself sounded this suspicion in his last book, *Answer to History*, and the Shah's officials whom I interviewed expressed similar sentiments. Moreover, additional information on the degree of American control over the Shah also shatters a larger myth—that the Shah of Iran, along with other rulers of the Middle East, had actually decided to raise the price of petroleum without first consulting the powerful consumer countries. The point here, however, is not to dwell on the intrigues of the international oil market but to illuminate the extent of American leverage over the Shah.

Quite frankly, it is difficult if not impossible to think of any sane advice or program of action that might have saved the Shah at the end. But then the whole purpose of such advice should have been to avoid the Shah's predicament rather than to attempt to deal with it after the fact. With the benefit of historical hindsight, and without stretching the limits of foreign policy beyond reason, it may be suggested that the United States had a vested interest in, and ample opportunities and adequate leverage for, compelling the Shah to clean up his act—to curb the corruption of the royal family, to spend more on social reforms instead of social events, to buy more tractors instead of tanks, and, above all, to balance political control with the need for political participation.

The above prescription, though reminiscent of the familiar clichés of development studies, was actually once imposed upon the Shah by an American president who understood both America's global responsibilities and the requirements of managing Third World countries. By the Shah's own admission, so disgusted was President Kennedy with the pervasive corruption in Iran that he demanded the appointment of a new prime minister before approving American economic assistance. By tying American aid to the introduction of comprehensive development programs, President Kennedy compelled the Shah to implement land reforms and other social programs that, if they had been administered properly in the subsequent years, might have saved the Shah from himself and spared America much aggravation. Unfortunately, John F. Kennedy's presidency was brief. And as the following pages shall reveal, neither his predecessors nor his successors demonstrated his keen intelligence and foresight in dealing with the Shah of Iran.

During the Truman administration, particularly in the immediate aftermath of the Azerbaijan crisis, the United States was the most admired nation in Iran. This was indeed conducive to a constructive American involvement in rebuilding Iran's war-torn economy. But the United States' commitment was largely confined to Iran's protection from direct Soviet attack. The Truman administration was also unprepared to supervise the expenditure of American economic aid to Iran. As a result, the Shah used the money to silence his soldiers and officials, while leaving the civilians to fend for themselves.

The benevolent image of the United States persisted nevertheless, a factor that later prompted the Iranian nationalists to seek American assistance in their crusade against the British AIOC. However, Truman and his advisors failed to appreciate the extent of public discontent in Iran that led to the rise of Dr. Musaddiq. By the time the Truman administration made a serious effort to settle the Anglo-Iranian disputes, it was already too late. The volatile mixture of nationalism and petroleum had already started the "prairie fire" that was later presented to the Eisenhower administration.

Judged by any standards, American participation in the overthrow of Musaddiq was a daring and dangerous adventure. Yet, after committing this act, the Eisenhower administration allowed the greed of international oil companies to dictate American policies. In doing so, these companies were permitted to approach their target, not as knowledgeable farmers collect their harvest, but as locusts attack and destroy an entire landscape. Instead of taking a handsome profit and leaving something behind for the local inhabitants, the oil companies looted Iran by stripping from her all rights concerning the production and marketing of her petroleum, by obligating the bankrupt Iranian treasury to pay large sums in compensation to the AIOC, and by making Iran dependent upon the "goodwill" of the oil companies for future revenues. Moreover, Eisenhower and his advisors chose to praise the Shah while ignoring the very factors that had necessitated American intervention to keep him in power. In retrospect, and considering the long-term American interest in controlling Iran, the strategy of the Eisenhower administration may be viewed as shortsighted and counterproductive.

The responsibility of the Eisenhower administration, however, should not be stretched to embrace all the sources of later trouble in Iran. The transformation of the Shah from an insecure young man to a ruthless dictator was conditioned by a web of factors related to both the Persian political culture and the policies of Eisenhower's successors. The story of the Shah bears a marked resemblance to Kipling's tale of "The Man Who Would Be King"—in which visions of power induce a man to ignore the reality of his predicament until it is too late. Much as the Kipling character was persuaded to regard himself as a descendant of Alexander the Great, the Shah was told by those surrounding him that he was indeed a reincarnation of Cyrus the Great and the shadow of God on earth. So alluring was the delusion, and so susceptible was the Shah to believing it, that he declared himself "The King of Kings and the Light of Aryan People."

For their part, and with the exception of John F. Kennedy, every

American president from Truman to Carter overlooked the internal problems of Iran and bestowed lavish praise upon the Shah. The process reached its zenith during the Nixon-Kissinger era, when the Shah was made the official "sheriff" of the Middle East, with King Hussein of Jordan and, later, Sadat of Egypt acting as deputy sheriffs, and with Saudi Arabia playing the role of local banker. Both the Shah and the Saudi royal family were encouraged—at least not discouraged—to "recycle" good portions of their oil revenue by buying military hardware. The Saudis transferred billions of dollars to international arms merchants to furnish "moderate Arabs" with guns and bullets, while the Shah used Iran's oil revenue to acquire the most sophisticated weaponry at a time when his people needed basic medical care, housing, and farming equipment.

To boost the Shah's ego, a contingent of American officials headed by Vice President Spiro Agnew, along with a supporting cast of European leaders, journeyed to Persepolis to join the Shah's celebration of twenty-five hundred years of Persian monarchy. The American media, generally reflecting the official line of policy, portrayed a most positive image of the Shah's regime. From Hollywood to Wall Street, Iran was hailed as an "island of stability" and a "center of civilization." Even the American academic community got into the act by offering the Shah and the members of his family honorary doctorates at the most prestigious universities. The Shah was simply overwhelmed by the continuous shower of compliments and believed that Iran was becoming a powerful industrial state, or what he called "Asian Germany." The Shah also grew increasingly intolerant of criticism. Consequently, any Iranian citizen who dared to question the wisdom of his policies was labeled as either "Marxist," "terrorist," "Muslim fanatic," or any combination of the above, and was subjected to punishments ranging from imprisonment to torture and execution. Nevertheless, by receiving good reviews in the United States, the Shah was perceived by the American public as a "moderate" Third World leader.

It was not until the mid-1970s that the majority of the Shah's subjects became convinced that "the emperor wore no clothes." By then, the Shah was so removed from reality that he failed to read the rage of his people. The eruption of this rage in 1978 caught the Shah and his friends by surprise because they had forgotten that there are limits to the endurance of any society and that management of Third World countries requires constant awareness and accommodation of such limits. At the hour of reckoning, the Shah looked around for advice and discovered that the yes-men surrounding him only shared his confusion. No less confusing were the signals coming from Washington, for it appeared that the Carter administration was encouraging the Shah to introduce liberal reforms amid the revolutionary chaos of Iran. The ailing Shah was then desperate enough to spend his very last days in Iran conferring with King Hussein of Jordan. In the end, as was the case in 1953, the Shah left Iran hoping for yet another miracle that would allow him to regain power. But this time, the magnitude of social upheaval in Iran was simply overwhelming, and the CIA could not even attempt to fix the problem with another "Operation Ajax."

If and when the complete record of American-Iranian relations during the Shah's era becomes accessible, it may show that the Shah was as much a victim as the executioner he was made out to be, and that his people turned against him because he reminded them of their subjugation, of their confusion, and of their inability to command genuine respect from the outside world. Similarly, if and when the full story of the Shah's era is told, it may exonerate President Carter from accusations that he was responsible for the loss of American influence in Iran. In fact, it may reveal that America's setback in Iran was occasioned, not so much because of the mistakes of the Carter administration, but because of the long years of mismanagement of American policies in that country.

This perspective, of course, postulates that American leaders could have and should have been more forceful in persuading the Shah to implement serious economic and political reforms of the variety suggested by President Kennedy. To an informed reader this prescription may reveal a tremendous grasp of the obvious. Nevertheless, anything along the lines of such a prescription often elicits negative responses from both liberals and conservatives. For most liberals, the prospect of imposing social reform on the Third World is improper if not immoral. The standard conservative reaction is to regard these prescriptions as hurling clichés at problems that have proven intractable in the face of strenuous efforts by persons of intelligence and dedication. Both sides might have a legitimate concern. But what liberals tend to forget is that imperial order by definition imposes a responsibility upon the patron to guide selected clients. And what conservatives seem to overlook is that such prescriptions have lasted long enough to become clichés because no one has come up with better ideas to replace them.

Whether liberals or conservatives have the better of the argument is a matter of profound indifference. The issue here is not moral bravery or intellectual originality. It concerns the awareness that the destiny of the Third World is determined by the race between reform and revolution. It refers to the recognition that America's interests are threatened as much, if not more, by the internal blemishes of the Third World as they are by the Communist penetration of these countries. And, finally, it relates to America's resolve in compelling her Third World allies to seek remedies for their appalling political and social inequities. This may not be on either the liberal or the conservative agenda. But it must be on America's agenda if she wishes to remain an imperial power and to play that role with efficiency and grace.

Any useful speculation about the future of American involvement in world affairs, however, must account for the perceptions of the American people regarding their relative security and economic power and their capacity to protect them. From all indications, it appears that the one universal American religion—faith in the future—has played a most active role in recent years in helping the American people to efface the traumas of Vietnam and Watergate and to forget Jimmy Carter's fretful analysis in the summer of 1979 that there was a crisis of confidence in the nation. In moving forward, the American people have been eager to revert to the enthusiasm and buoyancy of the immediate post–World War II era, when Dean Acheson made the remark that the United States was the only nation capable of grabbing hold of history and making it conform.

The prevailing mood of optimism in the United States, if supported by tangible results, will be most welcome news for Third World societies as well. A confident America may make a more reliable patron, if not a better partner, for the Third World countries. A prosperous America may be more charitable in aiding the poor nations. A secure America may view the defiance of the Third World not always as a sign of enmity but also as a psychological necessity nurtured by tired traditions and despair. Finally, a self-assured American leadership may be more inclined to remember what Winston Churchill recommended in his Nobel Prize address: "Let us therefore confront the clatter and rigidity we see around us with tolerance, variety and calm."

Notes

CHAPTER 1

1. For background on American perceptions of world affairs, see Robert E. Osgood, *Ideals and Self-interest in America's Foreign Relations* (Chicago, 1953); Albert K. Weinberg, *Manifest Destiny: A Study of National Expansionism in American History* (Baltimore, 1935); Dexter Perkins, *A History of the Monroe Doctrine* (Boston, 1963); Paul A. Varg, *Foreign Policies of the Founding Fathers* (East Lansing, Michigan, 1963).

2. The Annual Message to the Congress, 6 January 1941, *The Public Papers and Addresses of Franklin D. Roosevelt, 1940* 9:663–78.

3. For background on Russia's political heritage, see Nicholas V. Riasanovsky, *A History of Russia* (New York, 1977); Richard Pipes, *Russia Under the Old Regime* (New York, 1974); Hugh Seton Watson, *The Russian Empire, 1801–1917* (Oxford, 1967); Nicholas Berdyaev, *The Origins of Russian Communism* (Ann Arbor, Michigan, 1960).

4. W. Averell Harriman and Elie Abel, *Special Envoy to Churchill and Stalin* (New York, 1975), 275.

5. Milovan Djilas, *Conversations with Stalin*, trans. Michael B. Petrovich (New York, 1962), 114.

6. For Soviet propaganda efforts in Iran, refer to Chapter 3 of this book.

7. The reports by the Office of Strategic Services (OSS) and by American

diplomats from occupied territories such as Iran were indicative of American awareness of Soviet motives. See Chapter 3 of this book.

8. Thomas Powers, *The Man Who Kept the Secrets* (New York, 1979), 29.

9. Ibid., 28–29.

10. Cited by John Lewis Gaddis, *Strategies of Containment* (New York, 1982), 3.

11. James A. Nathan and James K. Oliver, *United States Foreign Policy and World Order* (New York, 1976), 25.

12. Arnold J. Toynbee, *America and the World Revolution* (New York, 1962), 97–102.

13. John Lukacs, *A History of the Cold War* (Garden City, New York, 1962), 3.

14. Vojtech Mastny, *Russia's Road to the Cold War* (New York, 1979), 307–13.

15. John Lewis Gaddis, *The United States and the Origins of the Cold War* (New York, 1972), 133–73.

16. Arthur M. Schlesinger, jr., "Origins of the Cold War," *Foreign Affairs* 46 (October 1967): 23.

17. Norman Graebner, "Cold War Origins and the Continuing Debate: A Review of Recent Literature," *Conflict Resolution* 13 (1 November 1969). I have borrowed heavily from this survey to present the status of the literature at the end of the 1960s.

18. Robert W. Tucker, *The Radical Left and American Foreign Policy* (Baltimore and London, 1971), 27–28.

19. Ibid., 29–33.

20. Ibid., 36.

21. Walter Lafeber, *America, Russia, and the Cold War, 1945–1966* (New York, 1967), 6–20.

22. Gabriel Kolko, *The Politics of War: The World and the United States* (New York, 1968), 624–25.

23. Tucker, op. cit., 97.

24. Noam Chomsky, *American Power and the New Mandarins* (New York, 1969), 399–400; Carl Oglesby and Richard Shaull, *Containment and Change* (London, 1967), 42; cited by Tucker, op. cit., 10.

25. Gar Alperovitz, *Atomic Diplomacy: Hiroshima and Potsdam* (London, 1965), 226–42.

26. Tucker, op. cit., 70.

27. Ibid., 148–49.

28. Ibid., 111.

29. Schlesinger, op. cit., 26–36.

30. Tucker, op. cit., 91–92.

31. Ibid., 93.

32. Ibid., 111.

33. Ibid., 73.

34. Ibid., 81.

35. Ibid., 151.

36. Ibid., 16.

37. Michael Harrington, *Socialism* (New York, 1972), 189–205.

38. Tucker, op. cit., 110–11.

39. William Appleman Williams, "Empire as a Way of Life," *The Nation* (2–9

August 1980); for a more detailed description of Williams's perspective, see *The Tragedy of American Diplomacy* (New York, 1959).

40. The presentation by John Lewis Gaddis was later published in the form of an article, "The Emerging Post-Revisionist Synthesis on the Origins of the Cold War," *Diplomatic History* 7, no. 3 (Summer 1983): 171–90.

41. Ibid., 189.

42. The topics relating to the Third World viewpoint are discussed in a wide range of literature, including political philosophy, sociology, comparative politics, political development, North-South dialogue, and theories of imperialism and intervention. There is no pretense that the summary of the Third World perspective presented in this chapter can adequately deal with every aspect of the literature. The intention, however, is to provide overviews of Third World arguments and to examine their validity.

43. Charles S. Maier, "Revisionism and the Interpretation of Cold War Origins," in *The Origins of the Cold War and Contemporary Europe,* ed. Charles S. Maier (New York and London, 1978), 20.

44. Ibid., 16–17.

45. Ibid., 17.

46. Toynbee, op. cit., 92–93.

47. Ibid., 93.

48. Ibid.

49. Robert A. Packenham, *Liberal America and the Third World* (Princeton, New Jersey, 1973), 358–59.

50. Jeane Kirkpatrick, "Dictatorships and Double Standards," *Commentary* (November 1979): 37–38. For an expanded view of this thesis, see Jeane Kirkpatrick, *Dictatorships and Double Standards* (New York, 1982).

51. Tucker, op. cit., 143.

CHAPTER 2

1. For two contrasting interpretations of the Monroe Doctrine, see Dexter Perkins, *The Monroe Doctrine, 1823–1826* (London, 1927); and William Appleman Williams, *The Contours of American History* (Cleveland, 1961).

2. For a description of missionary activities, see D. M. Finnie, *Pioneers East, The Early American Experience in the Middle East* (Cambridge, Massachusetts, 1967), 203–23.

3. Benson Lee Grayson, *United States–Iranian Relations* (Washington, D.C., 1981), 6–9.

4. R. K. Ramazani, *The Foreign Policy of Iran, 1500–1941* (Charlottesville, Virginia, 1966), 50.

5. George N. Curzon, *Persia and the Persian Question,* 1 (London, 1892), 391.

6. For a discussion of the treaty provisions, see Ramazani, op. cit., 39; also see J. C. Hurewitz, *Diplomacy in the Near and Middle East* (Princeton, New Jersey, 1956), 68–70.

7. Ramazani, op. cit., 38–40.

8. For discussion of the major provisions, see ibid., 77–78.

9. Ibid., 40–41.

10. Richard W. Cottam, *Nationalism in Iran* (Pittsburgh, 1964), 158.

11. Ramazani, op. cit., 42.

12. Ibid.

13. Ibid., 47.

14. Cottam, op. cit., 158.

15. Ramazani, op. cit., 47–49.

16. J. C. Hurewitz, *Middle East Dilemmas* (New York, 1953), 9.

17. Cited in Amin Saikal, *The Rise and Fall of the Shah* (Princeton, New Jersey, 1980), 12.

18. Raymond B. Fosdick, "Personal Recollections of Woodrow Wilson," in *The Philosophy and Policies of Woodrow Wilson*, ed. Earl Latham (Chicago, 1958), 44.

19. Woodrow Wilson, *The New Freedom* (Englewood Cliffs, New Jersey, 1913), 221.

20. Quoted in Arthur S. Link, *Wilson the Diplomatist* (Baltimore, 1957), 15.

21. This writer still has a vivid memory of a particular afternoon in a sleepy little town on the Caspian Sea near the Soviet border. Our history teacher in the first year of junior high school was something of a comic figure, a short and frail-looking man with a nervous twitch of the moustache. On that particular afternoon, he began to speak of Woodrow Wilson's idea of the League of Nations. His face lit up as he described President Wilson's affection and respect for humanity. Suddenly, he began to receive the attention of his students, and the nervous twitches of his moustache were no longer noticed. Savoring the rare attentiveness of the students, he spoke at length, going well beyond the class period. This was the one occasion when no one seemed eager to leave the classroom.

22. U.S. Department of State, *Foreign Relations of the United States, 1883* (Washington, D.C., 1884), 706. (Subsequently cited as *Foreign Relations.*)

23. Ibid.

24. *Foreign Relations, 1896*, 470. Also see Mehdi Heravi, *Iranian-American Diplomacy* (New York, 1969), 10–11.

25. *Foreign Relations, 1904*, 676–77; *Foreign Relations, 1905*, 722–27.

26. *Foreign Relations, 1907*, part 2, 941.

27. Ibid., 943.

28. For an excellent discussion of the Persian Constitutional Movement of 1906, see Laurence Lockhart, "The Constitutional Laws of Persia," *The Middle East Journal* 13, no. 4 (Autumn 1959): 377–88.

29. Edward Granville Browne, "The Persian Constitutional Movement," *Proceedings of the British Academy* 8 (London, 1917–18): 323–24.

30. *Foreign Relations, 1906*, 1217.

31. Cited in Heravi, op. cit., 21.

32. *Foreign Relations, 1911*, 685.

33. Ibid., 683.

34. Ibid., 684.

35. W. Morgan Shuster, *The Strangling of Persia* (London, 1913).

36. Robert E. Osgood, *Ideals and Self-interest in America's Foreign Relations* (Chicago, 1953), 27–28.

37. Alfred Thayer Mahan, "The Persian Gulf and International Relations," *The National Review* (September 1902): 37.

38. Ibid., 32.

39. Cited by Eric F. Goldman, *The Crucial Decade and After* (New York, 1960), 124.

40. For discussion of the provisions, see Ramazani, op. cit., 160–63; and Hurewitz, *Diplomacy in the Near and Middle East*, op. cit., 64–66.

41. An Address to a Joint Session of Congress, 2 April 1917, *The Papers of Woodrow Wilson, 1917* 41:519–27.

42. An Address to the Senate, 22 January 1917, *The Papers of Woodrow Wilson, 1916–1917* 40:533–39.

43. Heravi, op. cit., 44.

44. Bruce R. Kuniholm, *The Origins of the Cold War in the Near East* (Princeton, New Jersey, 1980), 133.

45. For discussion of the provisions, see Ramazani, op. cit., 187–89; see also Hurewitz, *Diplomacy in the Near and Middle East*, op. cit., 90–94.

46. Extracted from Shahrough Akhavi, *Religion and Politics in Contemporary Iran* (Albany, New York, 1980), 29.

47. Ibid., 29–30.

48. Heravi, op. cit., 52–58.

49. Mohammad Reza Pahlavi, *Answer to History* (New York, 1980), 67.

CHAPTER 3

1. Record Group (RG) 226, Office of Strategic Services (OSS) Report 75152, 16 May 1944, National Archives.

2. RG 59, Despatch 264, Department of State Decimal File 741.9111/69, 13 May 1942, National Archives. (Hereafter Department of State Decimal Files will be cited as DS followed by the appropriate number.)

3. Ibid.

4. RG 226, OSS Report 62227, 2 February 1944, National Archives.

5. RG 226, OSS Report 72668, 2 May 1944, National Archives.

6. Ibid.

7. *Ittilaat,* 25 April 1942.

8. RG 226, OSS Report 18220, 6 June 1942, National Archives.

9. RG 226, OSS Report 96500, Military Attache Report 3850, 14 September 1944, National Archives.

10. Ibid.

11. RG 226, OSS Report 58428, 30 January 1944, National Archives.

12. RG 226, OSS Report 44071, 16 September 1943, National Archives.

13. RG 226, OSS Report 80460, 26 May 1944, National Archives.

14. RG 226, OSS Report 53826, 21 December 1943, National Archives.

15. Ibid.

16. RG 226, OSS Report 80460, 26 May 1944, National Archives.

17. Ibid.

18. RG 226, OSS Report 52071, 28 December 1943, National Archives.

19. RG 226, OSS Report 96500, Military Attache Report 3850, 14 September 1944, National Archives.

20. RG 226, OSS Report 95263, 9 September 1944, National Archives.

21. RG 226, OSS Report 001061, Intelligence Report 6591, 23 September 1943, National Archives.

22. Ibid.

23. *Treaty of Alliance Between Great Britain, USSR and Iran* (London: H. M. Stationary Office, 1942).

24. Ibid.

25. For a description of treaties that the government of Iran had signed with European powers, see Chapter 2 of this book.

26. RG 226, OSS Report 000793, 6 September 1943, National Archives.

27. Ibid.

28. RG 59, Despatch 264, DS 741.9111/69, 13 May 1942, National Archives.

29. Ibid., Enclosure 2.

30. Ibid.

31. Mohammad Reza Pahlavi, *Answer to History* (New York, 1980), 71.

32. Ibid.

33. RG 226, OSS Report 17821, 26 May 1942, National Archives.

34. RG 226, OSS Report 000793, 6 September 1943, National Archives.

35. RG 226, OSS Report 25064, 12 October 1942, National Archives.

36. RG 226, OSS Report 28126, 5 January 1943, National Archives.

37. U.S. Department of State, *Foreign Relations of the United States, 1943*, vol. 4 (Washington, D.C., 1964), 429. (Subsequently referred to as *Foreign Relations.*)

38. RG 59, DS 891.00/2042A, August 1943, National Archives.

39. Ibid.

40. Ibid.

41. Pahlavi, op. cit., 72.

42. Ibid.

43. Ibid.

44. Ibid., 72–73.

45. *Foreign Relations, 1943*, vol. 4, 646–47.

46. RG 226, OSS Report 54425, 10 December 1943, National Archives.

47. RG 226, OSS Report 58428, 30 January 1944, National Archives.

48. RG 226, OSS Report L50478, December 1944, National Archives.

49. *Foreign Relations, 1944*, vol. 5, 470.

50. RG 226, OSS Report 107447, November 1944, National Archives.

51. Ibid.

52. Ibid.

53. Ibid.

54. RG 226, OSS Report 120559, 8 January 1945, National Archives.

55. RG 59, DS 861.9111/1-1045, 10 January 1945, National Archives.

56. RG 226, OSS Report 136077, 16 February 1945, National Archives.

57. RG 226, OSS Report 140059, 30 March 1945, National Archives.

58. RG 226, OSS Report L57135, 23 May 1945, National Archives.

59. RG 59, DS 891.00/8-2345, 23 August 1945, National Archives.

60. RG 59, DS 891.00/7-1445, 14 July 1945, National Archives.

61. RG 59, DS 891.00/9-2845, 28 September 1945, National Archives.

CHAPTER 4

1. U.S. Department of State, *Bulletin* (26 January 1953): 127.

2. U.S. Department of State, *Foreign Relations of the United States, 1946*, vol. 7 (Washington, D.C., 1969), 348. (Subsequently referred to as *Foreign Relations.*)

3. Harry S. Truman, *Memoirs: Years of Trial and Hope 1946–1952* (Garden City, New York, 1956), 95.

4. *New York Times*, 25 August 1957.

5. Harry S. Truman, *Truman Speaks* (New York, 1960), 71.

6. Herbert Druks, *Harry S. Truman and the Russians, 1945–1953* (New York, 1966), 125.

7. *New York Times*, 25 April 1960.

8. *Time Magazine* (28 January 1980): 13.

9. James A. Thorpe, "Truman's Ultimatum to Stalin on the 1946 Azerbaijan Crisis: The Making of a Myth," *Journal of Politics* 40 (February 1978): 193.

10. Ibid., 195.

11. Barry M. Blechman and Douglas M. Hart, "Afghanistan and the 1946 Iran Analogy," *Survival* 22 (November/December 1980): 252.

12. Ibid., 250.

13. For a description of Soviet tactics, see R. K. Ramazani, "The Autonomous Republics of Azerbaijan and Kurdish People's Republic: Their Rise and Fall," in *The Anatomy of Communist Takeovers*, ed. Thomas T. Hammond (New Haven, 1975), 448–74; also refer to Archie Roosevelt, Jr., "The Kurdish Republic of Mahabad," *The Middle East Journal* 1 (July 1947): 272–94.

14. For more information on the Tripartite Treaty, refer to Chapter 3.

15. For a description of Soviet activities in Iran, refer to Chapter 3.

16. James Byrnes, *All in One Lifetime* (New York, 1958), 331–34.

17. *Foreign Relations, 1946*, vol. 7, 293–94.

18. Ibid., 299.

19. Ibid., 300–301.

20. For information regarding both treaties, refer to Chapter 2.

21. James Byrnes, *Speaking Frankly* (New York, 1947), 123.

22. *Foreign Relations, 1946*, vol. 6, 694–96.

23. Ibid., 696–709.

24. George F. Kennan, *Memoirs: 1925–1950* (Boston, 1967), 295.

25. Byrnes, *Speaking Frankly*, op. cit., 254–55.

26. For the text of Byrnes's speech, see U.S. Department of State, *Bulletin* (10 March 1946): 355–58.

27. Ibid., 358; also see Byrnes, *All in One Lifetime*, op. cit., 349–50.

28. Truman, *Memoirs: Years of Trial and Hope 1946–1952*, op. cit., 94.

29. Cited by John Lewis Gaddis, *The United States and the Origins of the Cold War, 1941–1947* (New York, 1972), 307.

30. Ibid., 308–9.

31. Walter Bedell Smith, *My Three Years in Moscow* (Philadelphia and New York, 1949), 28–29.

32. Byrnes's preference for engaging public sentiment in foreign policy is well documented. For example, in *Speaking Frankly*, Byrnes devoted an entire section to this topic and concluded: "People can not act intelligently if, in all matters of importance affecting our relations with other governments, they are kept in dark. Let there be light—and lots of it!" (pp. 248–56). In regard to Iran, Byrnes specifically mentioned that publicizing Soviet activities played a vital role in influencing the outcome of events (pp. 250–51). Furthermore, the understanding that the note of March 6 was released to the press by design, and not because of an accidental news leak, is also indicated by John Lewis Gaddis (op. cit., 310).

33. For the text of the message, see *Foreign Relations, 1946*, vol. 7, 340–42.

34. Truman, *Memoirs: Years of Trial and Hope 1946–1952*, op. cit., 94–95.
35. Ibid., 95.
36. *Foreign Relations, 1946*, vol. 7, 340–48.
37. Blechman and Hart depicted the dispatch of the battleship *Missouri* as being completely irrelevant to the situation in Iran and argued, "that was connected to the situation in Turkey" (op. cit., 251). A look at a map of the Middle East, however, would indicate that Turkey is not as irrelevant to the Azerbaijan crisis as implied by Blechman and Hart. In fact, Robert Rossow, Jr., the head of the American consulate in Azerbaijan, described the presence of the battleship *Missouri* as a "pointed warning" to the Soviets. For the account of Rossow's interpretation, see "The Battle of Azerbaijan, 1946," *The Middle East Journal* 10, no. 1 (Winter 1956): 17–32.
38. *New York Times*, 13 and 14 March 1946; also cited by Bruce Kuniholm, *The Origins of the Cold War in the Near East* (Princeton, New Jersey, 1980), 323.
39. *Foreign Relations, 1946*, vol. 7, 356.
40. *Foreign Relations, 1946*, vol. 6, 716–17.
41. RG 59, DS 861.24591/4-1146, Telegram 510, National Archives; RG 59, DS 861.24591/4-1146, Telegram 315, National Archives.
42. RG 59, DS 891.00/11-246, Telegram 1430, National Archives; *Foreign Relations, 1946*, vol. 7, 356–66.
43. For the text of President Truman's press conference of 21 March 1946, see *Public Papers of the Presidents of the United States: Harry S. Truman, 1946* (Washington, D.C., 1962), 163–64. For the record of the Soviet announcement, see *Foreign Relations, 1946*, vol. 7, 378–79.
44. *Foreign Relations, 1946*, vol. 7, 407–27.
45. *Foreign Relations, 1946*, vol. 7, 348–49. This information was cited by R. K. Ramazani in 1971, by James Thorpe in 1978, and by Blechman and Hart in 1980.
46. *New York Times*, 25 April 1960. This evidence, perhaps the most interesting, is not even mentioned by Blechman and Hart. But it is cited by James Thorpe, op. cit., 191–92. It is also mentioned by J. Philipp Rosenberg, in an article that attempted to refute Thorpe's allegations, "The Cheshire Ultimatum: Truman's Message to Stalin in the Azerbaijan Crisis," *Journal of Politics* 41 (August 1979): 933–40.
47. Cited by Rosenberg, op. cit., 935–36.
48. Herbert Feis, *From Trust to Terror: The Onset of the Cold War, 1945–1950* (New York, 1970), 84.
49. Presidential appointment calendar, 23 March 1946, Harry S. Truman Library.
50. Smith, op. cit., 13–63.
51. Ibid., 47.
52. *Foreign Relations, 1946*, vol. 6, 733.
53. American Institute of Public Opinion, poll of 13 March 1946. Cited by Gaddis, op. cit., 315. According to this survey, 71 percent of those polled disapproved of Soviet policies, and only 7 percent expressed approval. Furthermore, 60 percent of the sample thought the United States was "too soft" toward Russia, and only 3 percent felt Washington's approach was "too tough."
54. Blechman and Hart, op. cit., 250.
55. Ibid., 249.
56. RG 59, DS 891.00/12-846, National Archives.

57. Smith, op. cit., 49–55.
58. *Foreign Relations, 1946,* vol. 7, 405–7; also see Kuniholm, op. cit., 326–37.
59. *Foreign Relations, 1946,* vol. 7, 441–42.
60. Ibid., 409.
61. Ibid., 421–31; for a more detailed presentation of American policies in the UN, see Kuniholm, op. cit., 303–50.
62. *Foreign Relations, 1946,* vol. 7, 453–59.
63. Ibid., 469–79.
64. Byrnes, *Speaking Frankly,* op. cit., 277–78.
65. For the text of Truman's address in Chicago on Army Day (6 April) 1946, see *Public Papers of the Presidents: Harry S. Truman, 1946* (Washington, D.C., 1962), 185–90; also see Gaddis, op. cit., 342; and Kuniholm, op. cit., 337.
66. U.S. Department of State, *Bulletin* (16 June 1946): 1045–47.
67. This party was formed on June 31, 1946. Also established on that same date was the "National Front," which later played an important role in the politics of Iran.
68. *Foreign Relations, 1946,* vol. 7, 500–517.
69. Ibid., 529–35.
70. Ibid., 551–52.
71. Ibid., 554–55.
72. Ibid., 556–60.
73. Ibid., 561.
74. RG 59, DS 891.00/12-2346, National Archives; RG 59, DS 891.00/12-1746, National Archives; *Foreign Relations, 1946,* vol. 7, 562–67. For a scholarly analysis of the disintegration of rebel regimes in Azerbaijan and Kurdistan, see Ramazani, op. cit., 471–74. For explanations regarding the Soviet failure to save these regimes, see Kuniholm, op. cit., 378–82.

CHAPTER 5

1. U.S. Department of State, *Foreign Relations of the United States, 1946,* vol. 6 (Washington, D.C., 1969), 709. (Subsequently referred to as *Foreign Relations.*)
2. For a description of Kennan's comment, refer to George F. Kennan, *Memoirs: 1925–1950* (Boston, 1967), 295.
3. James Byrnes, *Speaking Frankly* (New York, 1947), 302.
4. John Lewis Gaddis has argued that Kennan actually agreed with some aspects of Lippmann's argument but that Kennan's official status precluded public clarification of his views. Kennan later expressed his reservations in his memoirs. (See John Lewis Gaddis, *Strategies of Containment* [New York and Oxford, 1982], 26.) However, such an interpretation might be a loving treatment of Kennan's position, for throughout his distinguished career Mr. Kennan had perfected the method of speaking on both sides of the same issue without any apparent discomfort. An outstanding example of this behavior (which is explained later in this chapter) concerns Mr. Kennan's advocacy of the CIA's covert operations in 1948, which seemed to contradict his own advice expressed at the conclusion of his "long telegram" of 1946. Then, in the aftermath of Watergate, Mr. Kennan claimed that the CIA had not worked at all the way he had conceived it.

5. James A. Nathan and James K. Oliver, *United States Foreign Policy and World Order* (New York, 1976), 174–75.

6. Ibid., 175.

7. For a description of the OSS, see Richard Harris Smith, *OSS: The Secret History of America's First Intelligence Agency* (Berkeley, 1972).

8. Thomas Powers, *The Man Who Kept the Secrets: Richard Helms and the CIA* (New York, 1979), 25–31.

9. Stephen E. Ambrose and Richard H. Immerman, *Ike's Spies* (New York, 1981), 162–63; Smith, op. cit., 20.

10. Ambrose and Immerman, op. cit., 163; Powers, op. cit., 31; Smith, op. cit., 363–64.

11. U.S. Congress, Senate Select Committee on Government Operations with Respect to Intelligence Activities, *Hearings and Final Report*, book 4, 94th Cong. (Washington, D.C., 1976), S. Report 94-755, 6–13; Ambrose and Immerman, op. cit., 164–66.

12. Powers, op. cit., 35.

13. Ambrose and Immerman, op. cit., 168.

14. Powers, op. cit., 35–36.

15. Harry Rositzke, *The CIA's Secret Operations: Espionage, Counterespionage, and Covert Action* (New York, 1977), 186–87; Ambrose and Immerman, op. cit., 168.

16. Ambrose and Immerman, op. cit., 168.

17. Powers, op. cit., 37.

18. David Wise and Thomas Ross, *The Invisible Government* (New York, 1964), 96–97.

19. Powers, op. cit., 42–43.

20. Ibid., 43–44.

21. Ambrose and Immerman, op. cit., 170–75; Smith, op. cit., 367–68.

22. Powers, op. cit., 78–79.

23. Senate Select Committee Report, op. cit., 31–32; Ambrose and Immerman, op. cit., 176.

24. Powers, op. cit., 33.

25. Interview with Kermit Roosevelt, 1981.

26. *Washington Post*, 22 December 1963; cited by Ambrose and Immerman, op. cit., 167.

27. Senate Select Committee Report, op. cit., 31; Ambrose and Immerman, op. cit., 167.

28. Senate Select Committee Report, op. cit., 40; Ambrose and Immerman, op. cit., 178.

29. For an excellent discussion of Eisenhower's views, see Robert A. Divine, *Eisenhower and the Cold War* (New York and Oxford, 1981).

30. *Public Papers of the Presidents of the United States: Dwight D. Eisenhower, 1954* (Washington, D.C., 1954), 326; Divine, op. cit., 39.

31. Divine, op. cit., 11.

32. Ibid.

33. Ibid., 21.

34. Leonard Mosley, *Dulles* (New York, 1966), 391.

35. Ibid., 361.

36. For a brief description of the Eisenhower-Dulles attitude toward Third World nationalists, see Powers, op. cit., 91–115.

37. As cited by Ambrose and Immerman, op. cit., 188.

CHAPTER 6

1. The chronology of events is based on the recollections of Kermit Roosevelt as recorded in his book *Countercoup: The Struggle for the Control of Iran* (New York, 1979), and as described by Mr. Roosevelt during eight interviews with this author in 1980–81.

2. According to one account, the two men who approached the princess were Allen Dulles and Loy Henderson; see Leonard Mosley, *Power Play* (Baltimore, 1947), 414–15. But according to Kermit Roosevelt, the two men were Charles Mason and Gordon Somerset. In fact, Mr. Roosevelt has suggested that the reason Charles Mason was later removed from his post in Iran was that he indiscreetly talked about his relationship with the princess. See Roosevelt, op. cit., 145–46. Finally, according to Princess Ashraf, she met with an American and a Britisher who offered her money to make the trip to Tehran. Without mentioning their names, she has contended that she refused to accept the bribe but chose to go to Iran to help her brother. See Ashraf Pahlavi, *Faces in a Mirror* (Englewood Cliffs, New Jersey, 1980), 134–40.

3. Roosevelt, op. cit., 150–56.

4. The remark has been attributed to Kim Philby, the British agent who later became a Russian spy. During an interview in 1980, I asked Mr. Roosevelt what made him become involved in such activities. While acknowledging his personal predilection for intrigue, Mr. Roosevelt suggested that he accepted the assignment in Iran because the information available to him in 1953 seemed to indicate that the operation would benefit the United States, Great Britain, and Iran. But he also pointed out that, when Allen Dulles asked him to participate in overthrowing the government of Guatemala in 1954, he refused to accept the assignment because he felt unprepared for the task. Consequently, the job was given to other CIA operators, who accomplished the mission.

5. Roosevelt, op. cit., 156.

6. Ibid., 156–57.

7. Ray Carter to Eisenhower, 18 November 1952, Pre-Inaugural Papers; Herbert S. Parmet, *Eisenhower and the American Crusades* (New York, 1972), 477.

8. For a detailed description of concessions granted by the Persian government, see R. K. Ramazani, *The Foreign Policy of Iran, 1500–1941* (Charlottesville, Virginia, 1966), 65–72.

9. Ibid., 71.

10. An excellent survey of the APOC's activities is contained in a report by the Office of Intelligence Research of the State Department. See RG 59, Intelligence Report 5683, 6 March 1952, National Archives.

11. Analysis of the Constitutional Revolution of 1906 is presented in Chapter 2 of this book.

12. For a review of American oil interests in Iran, see Bruce Kuniholm, *The Origins of the Cold War in the Near East* (Princeton, New Jersey, 1980), 189–208.

13. Cited by Ramazani, op. cit., 208.

14. Kuniholm, op. cit., 191.

15. Intelligence Report 5683, op. cit., 2–4; Ramazani, op. cit., 250–57; Amin Saikal, *The Rise and Fall of the Shah* (Princeton, New Jersey, 1980), 22–23.

16. The public sentiment against this concession reached a new peak when Musaddiq became prime minister and publicly charged that the concession of 1933 was a fraud that preserved the British monopoly.

17. Kuniholm, op. cit., 91.

18. See Chapter 3 of this book.

19. See Chapter 3 of this book.

20. For an insightful survey of political events in Iran between 1945 and 1949, see Joseph J. Wagner, "Iran at the End of 1949," RG 84, 350-Iran, 16 January 1950, National Archives.

21. Intelligence Report 5683, op. cit., 8; Mohammad Reza Pahlavi, *Answer to History* (New York, 1980), 94; for a general background of the activities of international oil companies, see Anthony Sampson, *The Seven Sisters* (New York, 1975), 110–30.

22. The statement was made by Kashani during his conversations with Harriman in Tehran. See Vernon A. Walters, *Silent Missions* (New York, 1978), 255–56.

23. Ibid., 246.

24. Ibid., 247–51.

25. For example, see *New York Times,* 23 September 1951.

26. Anthony Eden, *Full Circle* (Boston, 1960), 199.

27. Paul Nitze, unpublished personal papers relating to Iran during 1950–53; made available to author by Mr. Nitze in 1980.

28. Ibid., Memorandum of conversation with Walter Levy, 2.

29. Princeton Seminars, 15–16 May 1954, Dean Acheson papers, 1607–8, Harry S. Truman Library.

30. Eden, op. cit., 198.

31. Ibid., 202.

32. The same magazine later declared that Ayatullah Khomeini was the symbol of evil on earth and selected him as Man of the Year in January 1980.

33. President Truman had decided that he was not going to seek another term in the November election of 1952.

34. Interview with Paul Nitze, 1980. The amount that the United States was willing to lend Iran had been reported to be as high as $100 million. But the figure of $50 million was indicated by Mr. Nitze.

35. Musaddiq to Eisenhower, 9 January 1953, and Eisenhower to Musaddiq, 10 January 1953. For the full text of the communications, see U.S. Department of State, *Bulletin* (20 July 1953): 76–77.

36. See note 7 of this chapter.

37. Interview with Paul Nitze, 1980. According to Mr. Nitze, "Foster [Dulles] was wrong about that and it was important to get a deal through with Musaddiq. It was in our interest, it was in the British interest, and it was in Iran's interest."

38. This topic is discussed later in the chapter.

39. Roosevelt, op. cit., 114–15.

40. Ibid., 120–23.

41. Ibid., 116.

42. Reports to Washington concerning Afghanistan indicated that the country "seems to be facing an imminent crisis which will determine for all time

whether it leans toward the West or becomes a Soviet satellite." See RG 320, 23 September 1951, National Archives.

43. RG 84, 350, 26 November 1952, National Archives.

44. National Intelligence Estimate, Document 64, part 2, 11 December 1952, Modern Military Headquarters Branch, National Archives.

45. RG 273, National Security Council 141, 19 January 1953, National Archives.

46. Robert H. Ferrell, ed., *The Eisenhower Diaries* (New York, 1981), 222–24.

47. Ibid., 192.

48. Eden, op. cit., 234–36.

49. Cited by Blanche Wilson Cook, *The Declassified Eisenhower* (New York, 1981), 178–79.

50. Musaddiq to Eisenhower, 28 May 1953, and Eisenhower to Musaddiq, 29 June 1953. For the text of the exchange, see *Public Papers of the Presidents of the United States: Dwight D. Eisenhower, 1953* (Washington, D.C., 1960), 482–86.

51. The general format of most National Security Council (NSC) and Joint Chiefs of Staff (JCS) documents of this period is based upon continual cross-references to earlier documents. Any attempt to trace the origins of an idea or plan of action is almost impossible because each preceding document is in turn linked to a set of yet earlier documents. The process may eventually guide a researcher not only to the creation of the NSC and the JCS but to the Creation! In fact, the NSC documents at times resemble religious literature, with declamatory statements regarding how the forces of "evil" shall be defeated. Considering that these documents were prepared for the presidents of the United States and not for the general public, the use of declamatory language and confusing format makes little sense, save for the possibility that the intention had been to prevent future historians from being able to link specific decisions to individuals or government agencies.

52. For the text of the JCS memorandum, see RG 218, JCS 1714/42, enclosure B, 31 October 1952, National Archives. For a record of JCS recommendations, refer to the following series of documents: JCS 1714/43, 5 December 1952 through JCS 1714/51, 25 August 1953; also refer to the proceedings of Joint Strategic Plans Committee (JSPC), including JSPC 961/17, 31 December 1952.

53. When referring to NSC 107/2 and NSC 136/1, the declassified JCS documents provide direct quotations of statements made by the NSC. But the same statements are deleted from the pages of declassified NSC documents. See RG 273, NSC 107/2, 27 June 1951, National Archives; RG 273, NSC 1361/1, 20 November 1952, National Archives.

54. RG 218, JSPC 961/24, 24 August 1953, National Archives; RG 218, JCS 1714/51, 25 August 1953, National Archives; RG 218, JCS 1714/52, 22 September 1953, National Archives. Also see the records of Chiefs Meetings, including: RG 218, Chiefs Meeting 18-53, 19 August 1953, National Archives; and RG 218, Chiefs Meeting 20-53, 20 August 1953, National Archives.

55. There were no official estimates regarding the number of casualties. The figure presented here is based upon interviews with several Iranians who claim to have witnessed the events in the streets of Tehran.

56. Roosevelt, op. cit., 206–7.

57. Ramazani, op. cit., 264–67; Mosley, op. cit., 219–20; Robert A. Divine,

Eisenhower and the Cold War (New York, 1981), 77–78; Robert Engler, *The Politics of Oil: A Study of Private Power and Democratic Directions* (New York, 1961), 207–9.

58. U.S. Department of State, *Bulletin* 31, no. 790 (16 August 1954); Ramazani, op. cit., 268–69; Eisenhower to Shah, 4 August 1954, and Shah to Eisenhower, 9 August 1954. For the text of the exchange, see *Public Papers of the Presidents of the United States: Dwight D. Eisenhower, 1954* (Washington, D.C., 1961), 688–89.

59. Interview with Kermit Roosevelt, 1981.

Bibliography

PRIMARY SOURCES

A. National Archives

Record Group 59, State Department Decimal Files:
891   (Internal Affairs of Iran)
711.91 (U.S.-Iranian Relations)
711.61 (U.S.-Soviet Relations)
711.41 (U.S.-British Relations)
761.91 (Britain-Iran Relations)
123   (Personnel Files of State Department Officials)
Record Group 84, Records of Foreign Service Posts (Iran, Iraq, Saudi Arabia, Turkey, Egypt, Afghanistan).
Record Group 273, National Security Council Documents.
Record Group 218, Joint Chiefs of Staff Documents.
Central Intelligence Agency, Collection of Documents in the Modern Military Headquarters Branch.
Record Group 226, Office of Strategic Services, Reports of Research and Analysis Branch.

B. Personal Papers and Official Publications

Acheson, Dean. Harry S. Truman Library. Independence, Missouri.

Dulles, John Foster. Princeton University Library. Princeton, New Jersey.

Henderson, Loy. Oral History Research Office. Columbia University, New York.

Nitze, Paul. Unpublished personal papers relating to Iran during 1950–53. Made available to this writer by Mr. Nitze in 1980.

The Papers of Woodrow Wilson, 1916–1917. Vol. 40. Princeton, New Jersey, 1982.

The Papers of Woodrow Wilson, 1917. Vol. 41. Princeton, New Jersey, 1983.

Public Papers and Addresses of Franklin D. Roosevelt, 1940. New York, 1941.

Public Papers of the Presidents of the United States: Harry S. Truman, 1946. Washington, D.C., 1962.

Public Papers of the Presidents of the United States: Dwight D. Eisenhower, 1953. Washington, D.C., 1960.

Public Papers of the Presidents of the United States: Dwight D. Eisenhower, 1954. Washington, D.C., 1960.

Treaty of Alliance Between Great Britain, USSR and Iran. London, 1942.

United Nations. *United Nations Security Council Journal.* First Year, Series 1, Meetings 1–42 (17 January–26 June 1946). New York, 1946.

——. *United Nations Security Council Official Records.* First Year, Series 2, Meetings 50–88 (10 July–31 December 1946). New York, 1946.

U.S. Department of State. *Foreign Relations of the United States, 1883.* Washington, D.C., 1884.

——. *Foreign Relations of the United States, 1896.* Washington, D.C., 1898.

——. *Foreign Relations of the United States, 1904.* Washington, D.C., 1905.

——. *Foreign Relations of the United States, 1905.* Washington, D.C., 1906.

——. *Foreign Relations of the United States, 1906.* Part 2. Washington, D.C., 1909.

——. *Foreign Relations of the United States, 1907.* Part 2. Washington, D.C., 1910.

——. *Foreign Relations of the United States, 1911.* Washington, D.C., 1918.

——. *Foreign Relations of the United States, 1940.* Vol. 3. Washington, D.C., 1958.

——. *Foreign Relations of the United States, 1942.* Vol. 4. Washington, D.C., 1963.

——. *Foreign Relations of the United States, 1943.* Vol. 4. Washington, D.C., 1964.

——. *Foreign Relations of the United States, 1944.* Vol. 5. Washington, D.C., 1966.

——. *Foreign Relations of the United States, 1945.* Vol. 8. Washington, D.C., 1969.

——. *Foreign Relations of the United States, 1946.* Vol. 6. Washington, D.C., 1969.

——. *Foreign Relations of the United States, 1946.* Vol. 7. Washington, D.C., 1969.

U.S. House of Representatives. Committee on Foreign Affairs. Subcommittee on Near East and South Asian Affairs. *United States Interests in and Policy Towards the Persian Gulf.* Washington, D.C., 1972.

——. Committee on International Relations. *The Persian Gulf 1975: The Continuing Debate on Arms Sales.* Washington, D.C., 1975.

——. Committee on Standards and Official Conduct. *Report of the Staff Study of Alleged Misconduct by Members of the House of Representatives Involving the Former Government of Iran.* Washington, D.C., 1979.

U.S. Senate. Committee on Foreign Relations. *Executive Sessions of the Senate Foreign Relations Committee.* 82d Cong., 1st sess., 1952. Vol. 3, part 2. Washington, D.C., 1976.

——. *Executive Sessions of the Senate Foreign Relations Committee.* 82d Cong., 2d sess., 1952. Vol. 4. Washington, D.C., 1976.

——. *Executive Sessions of the Senate Foreign Relations Committee.* 83d Cong., 1st sess., 1953. Vol. 5. Washington, D.C., 1977.

——. *Executive Sessions of the Senate Foreign Relations Committee.* 83d Cong., 2d sess., 1954. Vol. 6. Washington, D.C., 1977.

——. *The International Petroleum Cartel, the Iranian Consortium, and U.S. National Security.* Washington, D.C., 1974.

——. *United States Military Sales to Iran.* Washington, D.C., 1976.

——. Senate Select Committee on Government Operations with Respect to Intelligence Activities. *Hearing and Final Report.* Book 4, 94th Cong. Washington, D.C., 1976. S. Rept. 94-755.

BOOKS

Acheson, Dean. *Present at the Creation.* New York, 1969.

Akhavi, Shahrough. *Religion and Politics in Contemporary Iran.* Albany, New York, 1980.

Alexander, Yonah, and Allen Nanes, eds. *The United States and Iran: A Documentary History.* Frederick, Maryland, 1980.

Almond, Gabriel, and James Coleman. *The Politics of the Developing Areas.* Princeton, New Jersey, 1960.

Alperovitz, Gar. *Atomic Diplomacy: Hiroshima and Potsdam.* London, 1965.

Ambrose, Stephen E., and Richard H. Immerman. *Ike's Spies.* New York, 1981.

Arfa, Hassan. *Under Five Shahs.* London, 1964.

Barnet, Richard J. *Intervention and Revolution: The United States in the Third World.* New York, 1968.

Berdyaev, Nicholas. *The Origins of Russian Communism.* Ann Arbor, Michigan, 1960.

Bohlen, Charles E. *Witness to History 1929–1969.* New York, 1973.

Bullock, Alan. *Ernest Bevin: Foreign Secretary.* New York, 1983.

Byrnes, James. *Speaking Frankly.* New York, 1947.

——. *All in One Lifetime.* New York, 1958.

Chomsky, Noam. *American Power and the New Mandarins.* New York, 1969.

Chubin, Shahram, and Sepehr Zabih. *The Foreign Relations of Iran: A Developing State in a Zone of Great-Power Conflict.* Berkeley, California, 1974.

Cook, Blanche Wilson. *The Declassified Eisenhower.* New York, 1981.

Cottam, Richard W. *Nationalism in Iran.* Pittsburgh, 1964.

Curzon, George N. *Persia and the Persian Question.* London, 1892.

Dallek, Robert. *Franklin D. Roosevelt and American Foreign Policy, 1933–1945.* New York, 1979.

De Novo, John. *American Interests and Policies in the Middle East: 1900–1939.*

Minneapolis, 1963.

Divine, Robert A. *Eisenhower and the Cold War.* New York and Oxford, 1981.

Djilas, Milovan. *Conversations with Stalin.* Trans. Michael B. Petrovich. New York, 1962.

Druks, Herbert. *Harry S. Truman and the Russians, 1945–1953.* New York, 1966.

Dulles, Allen. *The Craft of Intelligence.* New York, 1963.

Dulles, John Foster. *War and Peace.* New York, 1950.

Eden, Anthony. *Full Circle.* Boston, 1960.

Eisenhower, Dwight D. *Mandate for Change.* New York, 1963.

Engler, Robert. *The Politics of Oil: A Study of Private Power and Democratic Directions.* New York, 1961.

Fanon, Frantz. *The Wretched of the Earth.* Harmondsworth, 1967.

Feis, Herbert. *From Trust to Terror: The Onset of the Cold War, 1945–1950.* New York, 1970.

Ferrell, Robert H., ed. *The Eisenhower Diaries.* New York, 1981.

Finnie, D. M. *Pioneers East: The Early American Experience in the Middle East.* Cambridge, Massachusetts, 1967.

Fontaine, Andre. *History of the Cold War: From the October Revolution to the Korean War, 1917–1950.* Translated by D. D. Paige. New York, 1968.

Fosdick, Raymond B. "Personal Recollections of Woodrow Wilson." In *The Philosophy and Policies of Woodrow Wilson,* ed. Earl Latham. Chicago, 1958.

Frye, Richard. *Iran.* London, 1960.

Gaddis, John Lewis. *The United States and the Origins of the Cold War, 1941–1947.* New York, 1972.

——. *Strategies of Containment.* New York, 1982.

Girling, John L. S. *America and the Third World.* London, 1980.

Goldman, Eric F. *The Crucial Decade and After.* New York, 1960.

Goldschmidt, Arthur, Jr. *A Concise History of the Middle East.* Boulder, Colorado, 1979.

Grayson, Benson Lee. *United States–Iranian Relations.* Washington, D.C., 1981.

Gurr, Ted Robert. *Why Men Rebel.* Princeton, New Jersey, 1970.

Halliday, Fred. *Iran: Dictatorship and Development.* New York, 1979.

Hammond, Thomas T., ed. *The Anatomy of Communist Takeovers.* New Haven, Connecticut, 1975.

Harriman, W. Averell, and Elie Abel. *Special Envoy to Churchill and Stalin.* New York, 1975.

Harrington, Michael. *Socialism.* New York, 1972.

Heravi, Mehdi. *Iranian-American Diplomacy.* New York, 1969.

Hoffmann, Stanley. *Primacy or World Order: American Foreign Policy Since the Cold War.* New York, 1978.

Huntington, Samuel. *Political Order in the Changing Societies.* New Haven, Connecticut, 1969.

Hurewitz, J. C. *Middle East Dilemmas.* New York, 1953.

——. *Diplomacy in the Near and Middle East.* Princeton, New Jersey, 1956.

Issawi, Charles. *The Economic History of Iran 1800–1914.* Chicago, 1971.

Kennan, George F. *Memoirs: 1925–1950.* Boston, 1967.

——. *Memoirs: 1950–1963.* Boston, 1972.

Khadduri, Majid. *War and Peace in the Law of Islam*. Baltimore, 1955.
——. *Political Trends in the Arab World*. Baltimore, 1970.
Kirkpatrick, Jeane. *Dictatorships and Double Standards*. New York, 1982.
Kolko, Gabriel. *The Politics of War: The World and the United States Foreign Policy 1943–1945*. New York, 1968.
Kuniholm, Bruce. *The Origins of the Cold War in the Near East: Great Power Conflict and Diplomacy in Iran, Turkey, and Greece*. Princeton, New Jersey, 1980.
Lafeber, Walter. *America, Russia, and the Cold War, 1945–1966*. New York, 1967.
Latham, Earl, ed. *The Philosophy and Politics of Woodrow Wilson*. Chicago, 1958.
Ledeen, Michael, and William Lewis. *Debacle: The American Failure in Iran*. New York, 1981.
Lenczowski, George. *Iran Under the Pahlavis*. Stanford, California, 1978.
Link, Arthur S. *Wilson the Diplomatist*. Baltimore, 1957.
Louis, William Roger. *Imperialism at Bay*. New York, 1978.
Lukacs, John. *A History of the Cold War*. Garden City, New York, 1962.
Maddox, Robert James. *The New Left and the Origins of the Cold War*. Princeton, New Jersey, 1973.
Maier, Charles S. "Revisionism and the Interpretation of Cold War Origins." In *The Origins of the Cold War and Contemporary Europe*, ed. Charles S. Maier. New York and London, 1978.
Marx, Karl. *A Contribution to the Critique of Political Economy*. New York, 1904.
Mastny, Vojtech. *Russia's Road to the Cold War*. New York, 1979.
May, Ernest. *"Lessons" of the Past: The Use and Misuse of History in American Foreign Policy*. New York, 1973.
Miller, Norman, and Rodrick Aya, eds. *National Liberation: Revolution in the Third World*. New York, 1971.
Millspaugh, Arthur. *Americans in Persia*. Washington, D.C., 1946.
Moore, Barrington. *Social Origins of Dictatorship and Democracy: Lord and Peasant in the Making of the Modern World*. Boston, 1973.
Mosley, Leonard. *Dulles*. New York, 1966.
——. *Power Play*. Baltimore, 1974.
Mottahedeh, Roy. *The Mantle of the Prophet: Religion and Politics in Iran*. New York, 1985.
Naipaul, V. S. *The Middle Passage*. London, 1962.
——. *An Area of Darkness*. London, 1964.
——. *A Bend in the River*. New York, 1979.
——. *Among the Believers*. New York, 1981.
Nathan, James A., and James K. Oliver. *United States Foreign Policy and World Order*. New York, 1976.
Nkrumah, Kwame. *Neo-Imperialism: The Last Stage of Imperialism*. New York, 1966.
Oglesby, Carl, and Richard Shaull. *Containment and Change*. London, 1967.
Osgood, Robert E. *Ideals and Self-interest in America's Foreign Relations*. Chicago, 1953.
Packenham, Robert A. *Liberal America and the Third World*. Princeton, New Jersey, 1973.

Pahlavi, Ashraf. *Faces in a Mirror.* Englewood Cliffs, New Jersey, 1980.
Pahlavi, Mohammad Reza. *Mission for My Country.* New York, 1961.
——. *Answer to History.* New York, 1980.
Parmet, Herbert S. *Eisenhower and the American Crusades.* New York, 1972.
Patterson, Thomas G., ed. *Containment and the Cold War.* Reading, Massachusetts, 1973.
Perkins, Dexter. *The Monroe Doctrine, 1823–1826.* London, 1927.
——. *A History of the Monroe Doctrine.* Boston, 1963.
Pipes, Richard. *Russia Under the Old Regime.* New York, 1974.
Powers, Thomas. *The Man Who Kept the Secrets: Richard Helms and the CIA.* New York, 1979.
Pruessen, Ronald W. *John Foster Dulles: The Road to Power.* New York, 1982.
Radhakrishnan, S. *Eastern Religions and Western Thought.* London, 1939.
Ramazani, R. K. *The Foreign Policy of Iran: A Developing Nation in World Affairs, 1500–1941.* Charlottesville, Virginia, 1966.
——. *Iran's Foreign Policy 1941–1973: A Study of Foreign Policy of Modernizing Nations.* Charlottesville, Virginia, 1975.
——. *The United States and Iran: The Patterns of Influence.* New York, 1982.
Riasanovsky, Nicholas V. *A History of Russia.* New York, 1977.
Roosevelt, Elliot. *As He Saw It.* New York, 1946.
Roosevelt, Kermit. *Countercoup: The Struggle for the Control of Iran.* New York, 1979.
Rositzke, Harry. *The CIA's Secret Operations: Espionage, Counterespionage, and Covert Action.* New York, 1977.
Rubin, Barry. *The Great Powers in the Middle East 1941–1947: The Road to the Cold War.* London, 1980.
——. *Paved with Good Intentions: The American Experience and Iran.* New York, 1980.
Said, Edward W. *Orientalism.* New York, 1978.
——. *Covering Islam.* New York, 1981.
Saikal, Amin. *The Rise and Fall of the Shah.* Princeton, New Jersey, 1980.
Sampson, Anthony. *The Seven Sisters.* New York, 1975.
Serfaty, Simon. *The Elusive Enemy.* Boston, 1972.
Shuster, W. Morgan. *The Strangling of Persia.* London, 1913.
Sick, Gary. *All Fall Down: America's Tragic Encounter with Iran.* New York, 1985.
Smith, Richard Harris. *OSS: The Secret History of America's First Intelligence Agency.* Berkeley, California, 1972.
Smith, Walter Bedell. *My Three Years in Moscow.* Philadelphia and New York, 1949.
Thucydides. *History of the Peloponnesian War.* Harmondsworth, 1954.
Toynbee, Arnold J. *America and the World Revolution.* New York, 1962.
Truman, Harry S. *Year of Decisions.* New York, 1955.
——. *Memoirs: Years of Trial and Hope 1946–1952.* Garden City, New York, 1956.
——. *Truman Speaks.* New York, 1960.
Tucker, Robert W. *The Radical Left and American Foreign Policy.* Baltimore, 1971.
——. *The Inequality of Nations.* New York, 1976.
Varg, Paul A. *Foreign Policies of the Founding Fathers.* East Lansing, Michigan, 1963.

Walters, Vernon A. *Silent Missions*. New York, 1978.
Watson, Hugh Seton. *The Russian Empire, 1801–1917*. Oxford, 1967.
Weinberg, Albert K. *Manifest Destiny: A Study of National Expansionism in American History*. Baltimore, 1935.
Williams, William Appleman. *The Tragedy of American Diplomacy*. New York, 1959.
———. *The Contours of American History*. Cleveland, 1961.
———. *Empire as a Way of Life: An Essay on the Causes and Character of America's Present Predicament*. New York, 1980.
Wilson, Woodrow. *The New Freedom*. Englewood Cliffs, New Jersey, 1913.
Wise, David, and Thomas Ross. *The Invisible Government*. New York, 1964.
Yergin, Daniel. *Shattered Peace: The Origins of the Cold War and the National Security State*. Boston, 1977.
Zabih, Sepehr. *The Communist Movement in Iran*. Berkeley, California, 1966.
Zonis, Marvin. *The Political Elite of Iran*. Princeton, New Jersey, 1971.

ARTICLES

Ajami, Fouad. "The Global Logic of the Neoconservatives." *World Politics* 30, no. 3 (1978).
———. "Third World Intervention: Orphans in Search of a Patron." *The Nation* 228, no. 22 (9 June 1979).
———. "The Fate of Nonalignment." *Foreign Affairs* 59, no. 2 (Winter 1980/1981).
Blechman, Barry M., and Douglas M. Hart. "Afghanistan and the 1946 Iran Analogy." *Survival* 22 (November/December 1980).
Browne, Edward Granville. "The Persian Constitutional Movement." *Proceedings of the British Academy* 8 (London, 1917–18).
Cottam, Richard. "The United States, Iran, and the Cold War." *Iranian Studies* 3, no. 1 (Winter 1970).
Gaddis, John Lewis. "The Emerging Post-Revisionist Synthesis on the Origins of the Cold War." *Diplomatic History* 7, no. 3 (Summer 1983).
Grady, Henry. "Real Story of Iran." *U.S. News and World Report* 31 (19 October 1951).
Graebner, Norman. "Cold War Origins and the Continuing Debate: A Review of Recent Literature." *Conflict Resolution* 13 (1 November 1969).
Halpern, Manfred. "Perspectives on U.S. Policy—Iran." *SAIS Review* 6, no. 3 (Spring 1962).
Hess, Gary R. "The Iranian Crisis of 1945–1946 and the Cold War." *Political Science Quarterly* 89 (March 1974).
Keddie, Nikki R. "The Iranian Power Structure and Social Change 1800–1969: An Overview." *International Journal of Middle East Studies* 2, no. 1 (1971).
Kirkpatrick, Jeane. "Dictatorships and Double Standards." *Commentary* 68, no. 5 (November 1979).
Lockhart, Laurence. "The Constitutional Laws of Persia." *The Middle East Journal* 13, no. 4 (Autumn 1959).
McFarland, Stephen L. "A Peripheral View of the Origins of the Cold War: The Crises in Iran, 1941–1947." *Diplomatic History* 4 (Fall 1980).

Mahan, Alfred Thayer. "The Persian Gulf and International Relations." *The National Review* (September 1902).

Maier, Charles S. "Revisionism and the Interpretation of Cold War Origins." *Perspectives in American History* 4 (1970).

Mark, Eduard. "Allied Relations in Iran, 1941–1947: The Origins of a Cold War Crisis." *Wisconsin Magazine of History* 59 (Autumn 1975).

Pfau, Richard. "Containment in Iran, 1946: The Shift to an Active Policy." *Diplomatic History* 1 (Fall 1977).

Ramazani, R. K. "Iran and the United States: An Experiment in Enduring Friendship." *The Middle East Journal* 30, no. 3 (Summer 1976).

Roosevelt, Archie, Jr. "The Kurdish Republic of Mahabad." *The Middle East Journal* 1 (July 1947).

Roosevelt, Kermit. "How the CIA Brought the Shah to Power." *Washington Post* (6 May 1979).

Rosenberg, J. Philipp. "The Cheshire Ultimatum: Truman's Message to Stalin in the Azerbaijan Crisis." *Journal of Politics* 41 (August 1979).

Rossow, Robert, Jr. "The Battle of Azerbaijan, 1946." *The Middle East Journal* 10, no. 1 (Winter 1956).

Ryan, Henry B. "A New Look at Churchill's 'Iron Curtain' Speech." *Historical Journal* 4 (1979).

Schlesinger, Arthur M., jr. "Origins of the Cold War." *Foreign Affairs* 46 (October 1967).

Shapiro, W. "Arming the Shah: Alms for the Rich." *Washington Monthly* 6 (February 1975).

Thorpe, James A. "Truman's Ultimatum to Stalin on the 1946 Azerbaijan Crisis: The Making of a Myth." *Journal of Politics* 40 (February 1978).

Watt, D. C. "The Persian Gulf—Cradle of Conflict." *Problems of Communism* 21 (May/June 1972).

Williams, William Appleman. "Empire as a Way of Life." *The Nation* 231, no. 4 (2–9 August 1980).

Young, T. Cuyler. "The Social Support of Current Iranian Policy." *The Middle East Journal* 6, no. 2 (1952).

Zabih, Sepehr. "Iran's International Posture: De Facto Non-Alignment Within a Pro-Western Alliance." *The Middle East Journal* 24, no. 3 (1970).

Zonis, Marvin. "Political Elites and Political Cynicism in Iran." *Comparative Political Studies* 1, no. 3 (1968).

NEWSPAPERS AND PERIODICALS IN PERSIAN

Akhbar-i Imruz [*Today's News*]. Library of Congress holdings: 21 April 1954–17 June 1954.

Asiya [*Asia*]. Library of Congress holdings: 22 June 1953–19 November 1953, 22–26 October 1961.

Besu-yi Ayandah [*Toward the Future*]. Library of Congress holdings: 13 June 1951–4 March 1953.

Dimiukrat-i Iran [*The Iranian Democrat*]. Library of Congress holdings: 24 October 1946–11 November 1947.

Ittilaat [*Information*]. Library of Congress holdings: 10 July 1926–December 1954.

Jabha-yi Azadi [Freedom Front]. Library of Congress holdings: 24 September 1950–3 May 1951.

Kayhan [The World]. Library of Congress holdings: 1 January 1943–31 March 1947, 1 June 1949–30 March 1954.

Mardum [The People]. Library of Congress holdings: 22 April 1943–30 June 1944, 1 January 1946–28 February 1946, 1 January 1947–30 September 1947, 25 June 1948–2 February 1949.

Mazandaran. [Named after a province in Northern Iran.] Library of Congress holdings: 19 September 1953–18 June 1954.

Muzakarat-i Majlis [Parliamentary Debates]. Library of Congress holdings: 1926–45.

Rahbar [The Guide]. Library of Congress holdings: 4 May 1943–21 November 1946.

Razm [Battle]. Library of Congress holdings: 11 May 1944–28 December 1944, 5 August 1948–16 October 1948.

Ruznamah-i Rasmi-i Kashvar-i Shahanshahi Iran [Official Gazette of the Imperial Government of Iran]. Library of Congress holdings: 1944–45, 1948–52.

Index